PRISON AREA,
INDEPENDENCE VALLEY

RE-MAPPING THE TRANSNATIONAL
A Dartmouth Series in American Studies

SERIES EDITOR
Donald E. Pease
Avalon Foundation Chair of Humanities
Founding Director of the Futures of American Studies Institute
Dartmouth College

The emergence of Transnational American Studies in the wake of the Cold War marks the most significant reconfiguration of American Studies since its inception. The shock waves generated by a newly globalized world order demanded an understanding of America's embeddedness within global and local processes rather than scholarly reaffirmations of its splendid isolation. The series Re-Mapping the Transnational seeks to foster the cross-national dialogues needed to sustain the vitality of this emergent field. To advance a truly comparativist understanding of this scholarly endeavor, Dartmouth College Press welcomes monographs from scholars both inside and outside the United States.

For a complete list of books available in this series, see www.upne.com.

Rob Kroes

PRISON AREA, INDEPENDENCE VALLEY

American Paradoxes in
Political Life and
Popular Culture

DARTMOUTH COLLEGE PRESS

HANOVER, NEW HAMPSHIRE

Dartmouth College Press
An imprint of University Press of New England
www.upne.com
© 2015 Trustees of Dartmouth College
Manufactured in the United States of America
Typeset in Sabon by Integrated Publishing Solutions, Grand
Rapids, Michigan.

For permission to reproduce any of the material in this
book, contact Permissions, University Press of New England,
One Court Street, Suite 250, Lebanon NH 03766; or
visit www.upne.com

Library of Congress Cataloging-in-Publication Data

Kroes, Rob.
Prison area, independence valley : American paradoxes in
political life and popular culture / Rob Kroes.
        pages   cm. — (Re-mapping the transnational)
Includes bibliographical references and index.
ISBN 978-1-61168-729-3 (cloth : alk. paper) — ISBN 978-1-
61168-730-9 (pbk. : alk. paper) — ISBN 978-1-61168-731-6
(ebook)
    1. United States—Civilization—21st century.   2. Political
culture—United States.   3. Popular culture—
United States.   4. United States—Politics and
government—2001–2009.   5. United States—Politics and
government—2009–   I. Title.

E169.12.K764 2015
306.097309'05—dc23

                                                        2014033139
5 4 3 2 1

CONTENTS

FOREWORD

Almost two hundred years ago, Alexis de Tocqueville determined to see America for himself and received a commission from the French government to study prison reform in the United States. His proposed study of prisons, of course, became a pretext for something much larger: a survey of American politics and society that became *Democracy in America*. The study of prisons brought Tocqueville to America. For Rob Kroes, one of Europe's most distinguished authorities on contemporary American culture, it was rather the other way around. For Kroes, it was his deep knowledge of American culture that brought him back to America and face to face with a couple of highway signs, Tocquevillian in their portent, that invited motorists to exit from Interstate 80 in Nevada toward a place called Independence Valley and to keep their eyes open for a "Prison Area." In this collection of essays, Kroes invites us to take these two signposts seriously for deepening our insights into America's cultural contradictions, especially how, after the September 11, 2001, attacks on the World Trade Center and Pentagon, the U.S. government's response to these attacks altered the meaning of America for Americans and Europeans alike.

Kroes's book is part of a long tradition of European commentary on the United States. His essays will certainly invite comparisons with Hector St. Jean de Crevecoeur, Alexis de Tocqueville, Charles Dickens, Frances Trollope, Matthew Arnold, and, more recently, Jean Baudrillard. But, whether consciously or not, Kroes's ironic and critical insights, and especially the lyricism of his prose, register more in the key of one of his Dutch forebears, historian Johan Huizinga. Best known for his *Waning of the Middle Ages*, Huizinga wrote two short books about the United States between the world wars, compiled into *America: A Dutch Historian's Vision, from Afar and Near*, about the significance of understanding the meaning of America's rapid modernization for European "Culture" and "Civilization." According to Huizinga, writing at the dawn of what Henry Luce called "The American Century," the United States had perfected the mechanization of life, gained the world, and lost its soul.

Kroes both echoes and updates Huizinga's insights in light of 9/11. For Kroes, it is the waning of the American Century, not of the Middle Ages, that merits our attention. And he brings years of expertise to the task of addressing the contradictions that beset contemporary America. Trained as a sociologist at Leiden University and the University of Amsterdam, Kroes, before accepting his current positions at Utrecht and Ghent universities, occupied the chair of American Studies at the University of Amsterdam and has written or edited dozens of books about American history, politics, and culture (especially photography). His writing has always been marked by a certain "reflexivity," an ability to talk about how and why he is adjusting his lens to capture the images passing in front of him. This book is no exception. He recalls the horror he experienced watching the 9/11 attacks and then the unfolding disbelief across much of Europe as the U.S. government launched a phony war against Iraq with untold consequences for America's political values at home and its credibility overseas.

How to explain America? For Kroes, culture matters. He opens his book with a deft examination of how President George W. Bush's ill-considered war against Iraq led many European intellectuals, including Kroes himself, to an "agonizing reappraisal" of the United States and its exercise of power in international affairs. This essay is followed by Kroes's assessment of Richard Drew's *Falling Man* and how this photograph achieved iconic status in conjunction with Don DeLillo's novel of the same name and Art Spiegelman's *In the Shadow of No Towers*. Never one to underestimate the complexities of cultural formations, Kroes invites us to think about the role of cultural productions in promoting America's rise to becoming a global power. Just when "empire as a way of life," as historian William A. Williams once put it, was taking hold in the United States, so were the musical idioms of jazz and Broadway musicals. Kroes's insights into the creativity of American musical formations are impressive, making clear that we always need to consider the possibility of "cultural reception being critically turned against its originator." Kroes's discussion of the interplay between production and reception, both linked by fundamental human wellsprings of imagination, will give scholars working in cultural studies pause for thought as they continue to grapple with how to understand popular culture and its cultural functions. Perhaps what is most compelling about these essays is this: they move readers beyond questions of "America" and "Americanization" into thinking more generally about the human condition (as in the case of Kroes's marvelous conclusion to his essay "Freaks on Display"). That understanding *what* we see, whether in a film like *Django Unchained* or in photographs taken of the Holocaust, helps make us *who* we are is a point Kroes is keen to drive home through these essays about the power of cultural representations. His deeply humane readings will force readers to examine their own frames of reference for thinking about the Holocaust and more recent iterations of racism and terrorism. His final essay about President Barack Obama and the responses to his presidency pulls together Kroes's interest in understanding the power (and limits) of cultural discourse to refashion America's image in the world after 9/11.

To sum up, *Prison Area, Independence Valley* takes us on a journey into what Huizinga (mistakenly) read as a cultural wasteland. Kroes invites us to take the exit with him from the interstate highway, to reflect on where and who we are, and then to continue our journey with a sense that no century is safe in the hands of just one nation.

Robert W. Rydell
Montana State University

PRISON AREA,
INDEPENDENCE VALLEY

INTRODUCTION

This is a Tocqueville meets Gandhi moment:
Democracy in America? It would be a good idea.
—Pierre Guerlain, *The Huffington Post,* October 10, 2013[1]

IN NEVADA, WHILE driving along U.S. Interstate 80, I saw two
road signs following each other in close order: "Prison Area,"
and "Independence Valley." The signs came as a shock. I instantly
realized that I had found the title for my new book. Between them
they seemed to capture poignantly the poles that my continuing
fascination with American life and culture had always moved between, like a perpetual-motion pendulum, never finding equilib-
rium, never coming to rest. Under the unforgiving Nevada sun,
the space around me had all of a sudden turned into a conceptual
space, where "independence" along with close conceptual asso-
ciates such as "freedom," "equality," and "democracy," found
themselves confined by a world view centering on imprisonment.
Conflicting faces of America had popped up in the middle of the
desert and kept riding along with me in the same way that the
sun and the moon move along with the long-distance traveler
while the surrounding landscape appears to rush by.

America a prison area? In many ways: yes. The country seems
infatuated with imprisoning its citizens, and increasingly so. The
United States has spent $300 billion since 1980 to expand its
prison system. It imprisons 2.2 million people, 25 percent of the

world's prison population. For every 100,000 adults in the country there are 742 behind bars. Some 5 million are on parole. Only 30 to 40 percent are white. Depending on the state, prisoners lose their political rights, including the vote, sometimes for life. This is a system of creeping disenfranchisement, weighted against the black population.[2] Another trend of equally ominous portent ties in with this: America now employs as many private security guards as high school teachers, nearly double their number in 1980. It is a trend that runs parallel to another one: the number of protective services employees tracks with America's growing inequality. In both respects the United States is ahead of all countries that we tend to think of as constituting the West, and increasingly so. As its inequality grows, so does the proportion of guard labor.[3] Yet, as I was pondering this behind the wheel, popular culture memories reminded me that some of the great sagas of rebellion and resistance against the spirit of incarceration, redeeming the inspirational lure of independence, come from America. There are many examples from American film history, but one came to my mind with particularly great force: *Runaway Train*.[4] Starting with an uprising of inmates against a tyrannical prison regime, it tells the story of one breakaway prisoner, an emblem of the unbreakable spirit of independence, on his way to the ultimate act of defiance, choosing liberty while racing toward certain death on his runaway train. Paradoxically then, prisons and their attendant images of chain gangs, watchtowers, barbed wire, and armed guards may take one back to an American inspirational repertoire of human agency and self-reliance.

America an independence valley, then? A safe haven, a refuge, extending a welcome to all those "yearning to breathe free," in Emma Lazarus's words as spoken by the silent lips of the mother of exiles—the Statue of Liberty—in New York Harbor? Again, in many ways: yes. Yet the welcome has increasingly become mixed in with a sense of threat, with distrust and suspicion. Tellingly, before getting to Independence Valley, Nevada, I had passed Camp Williams, near Bluffdale, Utah, between Utah Lake and Great

Salt Lake. It is the location for the new Utah Data Center, also known as the Intelligence Community Comprehensive National Cybersecurity Initiative Data Center, a mouthful but like nothing compared with the center's data storage capacity, estimated to be on the order of exabytes or higher. It is to serve as the ultimate repository for the continuing collection of Internet and telecommunication data, concerning U.S. citizens and foreigners alike. As Daniel Ellsberg, the father of all contemporary whistleblowers, has written, with sardonic wit, the U.S. government is realizing the ambition of the Stasi, the East German secret police, who wanted to know everything about everybody.[5] Following recent revelations by whistleblower Edward Snowden—now offered sanctuary in, of all places, Russia—it is hard to avoid the conclusion that they confirm the arrival of a full-fledged surveillance state to the United States. It is like a stealthy insurrection by the government against the spirit and letter of the law, and has proceeded apace, ever since 9/11, under both the Bush and Obama administrations.

Yet the threat of governmental invasion into the private sphere predates 9/11 and goes back to well before the exponential growth in computer data-mining capabilities. The following words eerily capture contemporary developments, yet were spoken in the 1970s:

> The [National Security Agency's] capability at any time could be turned around on the American people, and no American would have any privacy left, such is the capability to monitor everything: telephone conversations, telegrams, it doesn't matter. There would be no place to hide. [If a dictator ever took over, the N.S.A.] could enable it to impose total tyranny, and there would be no way to fight back.

These are words from one of the most admired and influential politicians among American liberals in the last several decades: Frank Church of Idaho, the four-term U.S. senator who served from 1957 to 1981. He was, among other things, one of the Sen-

ate's earliest opponents of the Vietnam War, a former chairman
of the Senate Foreign Relations Committee, and the chairman
of the committee (bearing his name) that in the mid-1970s in-
vestigated the widespread surveillance abuses committed under
every president since FDR. That was the investigation that led to
the enactment of FISA, the criminal law prohibiting the executive branch from intercepting the communications of American
citizens without first establishing "probable cause" and obtain-
ing a court warrant—the very law that the Bush administration
got caught violating and that was gutted by the Democratic-led
Congress in 2008, with the support of then-Senator Obama. The
abuses uncovered by the Church Committee also led to the enactment of further criminal prohibitions on the cooperation by
America's telecoms in any such illegal government spying, prohibitions that were waived away when the same 2008 Congress retro-
actively immunized America's telecom giants from having done so.

Much of what Senator Church had cautioned his fellow-
citizens about has since come to pass. Nor is this the only cloud
darkening Independence Valley. The train of associations that the
valley's name gets going includes freedom, includes equality. Like
independence, they are hallowed ideals, given protection in foun-
dational texts like the U.S. Constitution and figuring centrally in
America's national rhetoric. Yet, like independence, their actual-
ity is often a far cry from the ideal. They are besmirched almost
beyond recognition when coming from the mouth of a president
who, in the dismal chaos wrought by the 2003 American invasion of Iraq, could proudly see "freedom on the march." And
what sort of an ideal is equality when in fact the United States
has known a widening gap in wealth and income between its
higher and lower levels of society? As measured by the Organization for Economic Cooperation and Development (OECD), the
United States finds itself, with countries like Chile, Turkey, and
Mexico, near one end of the scale, with a wide and increasing
wealth gap, while many European countries are on the opposite
end. Yet the stark picture of a small top layer holding an obscene

concentration of wealth and income may be revolting but rarely leads people actually to revolt. Protest movements pitching their pitiable tents in city parks fizzle out with almost no trace left.

One could easily go on in this vein, uncovering one revolting face of the United States after another. Yet there is always the pull of precisely the opposite America, presenting faces that in carnivalesque ways instantly recast its identity. As the American historian Michael Kammen reminded us in the early 1970s, Americans are "a people of paradox." They refuse to live by the logic of any preconceived idea and, like the trickster or confidence man, blithely exchange one identity for another, leaving puzzled outsiders to sort out for themselves what is virtual and what real in their performance of a dizzying range of inventions. In their virtuoso multiplying of worlds, they virtually inhabit invented worlds as so many simulacra that turn the real world upside down and inside out, while producing incisive commentary on the fears and anxieties that run through their lives as they collectively live them. There is a redemptive, if not exhilarating, quality in this elan vital that has kept many observers of America spellbound.

This is a story that has kept repeating itself. Yet ever since the ominous day of 9/11 there has been an added urgency to following this story as it is unfolding, urging the observer to seek a new balance between feelings of revolt and fascination. In the many self-presentations that America offers to the world, more strongly than before the gloves have come off. America shows the naked face of a surveillance state and an imperial hegemon. Yet always it morphs endlessly into rival narratives, showing itself as the tragic hero, struggling to find mastery and control of his fate on a run-away train to ultimate doom.

Revulsion and fascination have been the poles that have kept me exploring the enigma of America over the last several years. This book offers the reflection of what is in many ways a personal quest, yet one that I hope will find sympathetic recognition among its readers.

THE GEORGE W. BUSH ADMINISTRATION
AND EUROPEAN ANTI-AMERICANISM

NOUS SOMMES TOUS AMÉRICAINS. "We are all Americans." Such was the rallying cry of Jean-Marie Colombani, editor-in-chief of the French newspaper *Le Monde*, published two days after the September 11, 2001, terrorist attack against symbols of America's power. He went on to say: "We are all New Yorkers, as surely as John Kennedy declared himself, in 1963 in Berlin, to be a Berliner." While Colombani himself evoked Kennedy's historic declaration for his readers, an even older use of this rhetorical call to solidarity may come to mind. It is Thomas Jefferson's call for unity after America's first taste of two-party strife. Leading the opposition forces to victory in the presidential election of 1800, he assured Americans that "we are all Republicans, we are all Federalists" and urged his audience to rise above the differences that many feared might divide the young nation against itself. Clearly, there would have been no need for such a ringing rhetorical call if there had not been an acute sense of difference and division at the time. The same could be said of Colombani's timely expression of solidarity with an ally singled out for a vengeful attack, solely because it had come to represent the global challenge posed by a shared Western way of life. An attack against the United States was therefore an attack against common values held dear by all who live by standards of democracy and the open society that it implies. But as in Jefferson's case, the rhetorical urgency of the call for solidarity suggested that there were differences and divisions to be transcended, or at least temporarily shunted aside. That sense of difference between the United States and its European allies had always been there during the Cold War, but it was contained by the threat of a common enemy. The end of the Cold War brought the felt need for a reorientation of strategic thinking on both sides of the Atlantic that, if anything, only sharpened differences and divisions.[1]

Many changes that occurred during the 1990s were direct consequences of the end of the Cold War and the Soviet Union's collapse. They would likely not have occurred without the breakdown of the international balance of power and ideology and of patterns of clientage that were typical of the Cold War world. Some of the obvious examples are the expansion of the European Union (EU) and of the North Atlantic Treaty Organization (NATO) into areas previously under the sway of the Soviet Union; the Balkan wars of the 1990s and Saddam Hussein's 1990 invasion of Kuwait. Most dramatically, perhaps, transatlantic tensions, never absent during the Cold War but contained by the imperative of a joint defense against the Soviet bloc, are now manifested as clashing visions of the post–Cold War new world order. The phrase "New World Order" was used by the elder George Bush during the first Gulf War, when briefly it seemed as if a framework of international institutions, centered on the United Nations, could finally come into its own. But the world has moved a long way from those early hopes and visions of global unity.[2]

Perhaps we should be asking ourselves a new question: Do the terrorist attacks on symbols of American power on September 11, 2001, represent a greater sea change than the end of the Cold War? Or were they merely the catalyst that led America to implement a foreign policy that had been in the making since the early 1990s? If the second scenario is true, and it seems likely that it is, then America's current foreign policy is clearly a response to its position as the single hegemon in a unipolar world, intent on safeguarding that position.

The origin of that policy was a Defense Planning Guidance document drafted in 1992 by Undersecretary of Defense for Policy Paul D. Wolfowitz at the behest of then Secretary of Defense Richard Cheney, entitled "The New American Century." In 1997 a group of neoconservative foreign policy analysts coalesced around the Project for a New American Century and founded a think-tank under that name. Their thinking hardened around a view that American foreign policy should center on military strength. When the George W. Bush administration entered office in 2000, those neoconservatives came into position to implement their views. Throughout the 1990s national rituals such as the Super Bowl increasingly blended mass spectator sports with displays of military prowess and martial vigor that paralleled the gestation of the new foreign policy views.[3] That trend may herald a militarization of the American public spirit, propagated through the mass media. To some the displays are eerily reminiscent of earlier such public spectacles, such as those at the 1936 Olympic Games in Nazi Germany. Those militarized rituals may have readied the American public for the later curtailment of democratic rights through the 2001 Patriot Act and the emergence of a national security state under the George W. Bush administration. In a 2004 article, the American philosopher Richard Rorty warned Europeans that institutional changes made in the name of the war on terrorism could bring the end of the rule of law in both the United States and Europe. Remarkably, he forgot to mention that many of those changes had already come to the United States, without much public debate or resistance.[4]

Much though the entire world may have changed in the wake of the Cold War, my focus shall be on the particular ways these changes have affected Europe and the United States, internally as well as in their transatlantic relationship. An important trend to notice is the way Europeans and Americans have begun to redefine each other, in response to a creeping alienation that has affected public opinion and discourse on both sides of the Atlantic. If each side increasingly sees the other as "Other," more alien than at any point during the Cold War, then the construction of this perspective is not entirely new. It draws on older repertoires of anti-Americanism in Europe and of anti-Europeanism in the United States, as illustrated by Secretary of Defense Donald H. Rumsfeld's snide reference to "Old Europe."[5] Yet there may be a new and more ominous ring to those revived repertoires because they may strike responsive chords among people who previously thought they were free of such adversarial sentiments.

In what follows I wish to explore that new resonance. It is partly a personal account, an attempt at introspection, tracing emotional and affective shifts in the way I perceive and experience America. Let me begin with a necessary proviso. In 2003, in *Le Monde*,[6] Alfred Grosser reminded us that one need not be labeled "anti-American" for opposing U.S. foreign policy, nor an "anti-Semite" or "anti-Zionist" for taking Israeli government policy to task. He is not the first to make that point, nor will he be the last. The point bears making time and time again. Too often the cry of anti-Americanism or anti-Semitism is used as a cheap debating trick to silence voices of unwelcome criticism. Like Grosser, I have studied forms of anti-Americanism for years, trying to understand both what triggers it and the logic of its inner structure, while looking at it from a rather Olympian height. More often than not anti-Americanism had seemed more meaningfully connected to the non-American settings where it appeared than to America itself. But like Grosser I now feel the need to make explicit a point that had for so long seemed obvious. He and I and many others now feel a strong urge to distance ourselves from the directions America's foreign policy is taking. Ironically we are now confronting the charge that we have become anti-American. What had been a topic of intellectual and scholarly interest has now assumed the poignancy of a private dilemma. Grosser and I and others know we have not turned

anti-American, even while we have become critical of the recent turns in American policies. We are now facing the question:
When does a stance critical of specific American policies become
anti-American? For the shift from criticism to anti-Americanism
to occur, more is needed than disagreements, however vehement,
over certain policies. Anti-Americanism typically proceeds from
specific areas of disagreement to larger frameworks of rejection,
seeing particular policies or events as typical of America more
generally. From that perspective anti-Americanism is mostly reduc-
tionist, seeing, for example, only the simplicity of the cowboy stereotype and the Texas provincialism in President George W. Bush's
response to terrorism, or only the expansionist thrust of American
capitalism in Bush's Middle East policies. Entire repertoires of ste-
reotyped Americas can be conjured up to account for any contemporary transatlantic disagreements. Later on I will return to these
repertoires, in their historical configurations, in greater detail.[7]

   To the extent that the topic of anti-Americanism has come home
to roost for people like Grosser and me, this essay is meant to explore how my involvement with the topic has changed in the wake
of September 11. It is in part a personal account of my attempts
to keep my feelings of alienation and anger over recent trends in
America's foreign policy from alienating me from America more
generally. It is the report of a balancing act. Or better perhaps: it
is an agonizing reappraisal,[8] for indeed my inner image of America has changed, affecting my sense of affiliation and closeness to
the country. *Before* that change I could study anti-Americanism
with sardonic joy and intellectual distance, but *now*, for the first
time, my insights have gained a new personal relevance, urging
me to reappraise my inner feelings in terms of their possible anti-
Americanism. That reappraisal is agonizing because, in my view
and that of many others, America—as much as the historically
contingent construct of anti-Americanism—has changed face.

   I happened to be in the United States on the dismal day of September 11, 2001. I had flown from Washington, DC, to Logan

Airport in Boston the previous evening, only hours before knife-wielding terrorists highjacked three airplanes that had taken off from Logan. I stood transfixed in front of the television screen, impotently watching the second plane crash into the second of Manhattan's Twin Towers, then seeing them implode—almost in slow motion, as I remember it. A year later I was back in the United States, watching how Americans remembered the events of the year before in a moving, simple ceremony. The names were read of all those who had lost their lives in the towering inferno of the World Trade Center. Their names appropriately reflected the image that the words "World Trade Center" conjure up; they were the names of people from all over the world, from Africa, the Middle East, the Far East, the Pacific, Latin America, Europe, and, of course, North America—people of many cultures and many religions. Again the whole world was watching, and I suddenly realized that something remarkable was happening. The American mass media recorded an event staged by Americans. Americans were powerfully reappropriating a place where a year before international terrorism had been in charge. They literally turned the site into a *lieu de mémoire*. They were, in the language of Abraham Lincoln's Gettysburg Address—read again on this occasion—consecrating the place. They imbued it with the sense and meaning of a typically American scripture. It was the ringing language of freedom and democracy that, for more than two centuries, has defined America's purpose and mission.

I borrow the words "American scripture" from Michael Ignatieff. He used them in a piece he wrote for a special issue of the British literary magazine *Granta*.[9] He is one of twenty-four writers from various parts of the world who contributed to a section entitled "What We Think of America." Ignatieff described American scripture as "the treasure house of language, at once sacred and profane, to renew the faith of the only country on earth . . . whose citizenship is an act of faith, the only country whose promises to itself continue to command the faith of people like me, who are not its citizens." Ignatieff is a Canadian.

He described a faith and an affinity with American hopes and dreams that many non-Americans share. Yet, if it was the point of *Granta*'s editors to explore the question of "Why others hate us, Americans," Ignatieff's view was not of much help. In the world outside the United States after 9/11, as *Granta*'s editor, Ian Jack, reminded us, there was a widespread feeling that Americans "had it coming to them," that it was "good that Americans now know what it's like to be vulnerable." For people who share such views, American scripture deconstructs into hypocrisy and willful deceit. They may well see their views confirmed now that America is engaged in an occupation of Iraq—advertised as an intervention to bring democracy—while in fact the United States carries out what may well be war crimes under the terms of international treaties that count the United States among their signers.

There are many hints from the recent past that people's views of America have been shifting in the direction of disenchantment and disillusionment. To be sure, there were fine moments when President Bush rose to the occasion and used the hallowed words of American scripture to make it clear to the world and his fellow Americans what terrorism had truly attacked: the terrorists' aim had been not just the destruction of symbols of American power and prowess but rather the destruction of the freedom and democracy that America sees as its foundation. Those were moments when the president literally seemed to rise above himself. But it was not long before he showed a face of America that had already begun to worry many longtime friends and allies during Bush's first year in office.

Even before September 11 the Bush administration had signaled its retreat from the internationalism that had inspired U.S. foreign policy since at least World War II. Ever since the administration of Woodrow Wilson, American scripture has also implied a vision of world order that would forever transcend the lawlessness of international relations. Many of the international organizations that now regulate interstate relations and give legitimacy to international actions bear a markedly American imprint and spring from American ideals and initiatives. The elder President Bush—in spite of his avowed aversion to the "vision thing"—nevertheless deemed it essential to speak of a new world order when, at the end of the Cold War, Saddam Hussein's invasion of Kuwait seemed to signal a relapse into international lawlessness. The younger Bush took a narrower, national-interest view of America's place in the world. With unabashed unilateralism he moved U.S. foreign policy away from high-minded idealism and the arena of international treaty obligations. He actively undermined the fledgling International Criminal Court in The Hague, rather than taking a leadership role in making it work. He displayed a consistent unwillingness to play by international rules and to abide by the decisions of even those international bodies that the United States helped to set up. He has squarely placed the United States above or outside the reach of international law, viewing himself as the sole and final arbiter of America's national interest.

After September 11 that outlook only hardened. The overriding tendency to view international relations from the perspective of the war against terrorism has led the United States to ride roughshod over both constitutionally protected civil rights and international treaty obligations under the Geneva Conventions in its handling of individuals—U.S. citizens among them—suspected of links to terrorist networks. Because President Bush saw antiterrorism efforts as the only way to define who is with America and who against it, he defended and justified forms of state terrorism—whether by Russia against the Chechens, or by Israel against the Palestinians—as antiterrorist efforts. He called Israeli prime minister Ariel Sharon a "man of peace," and preempted future negotiations between the Palestinians and the Israelis by supporting Israel's positions on the Palestinians' rights of return under international law, as well as on the Israeli settlement of occupied Palestinian land, which is against international law. When Europeans disagreed with those policies and wished to take a more balanced view of the Israeli-Palestinian conflict, the Bush administration and many op-ed voices in the United States attributed the dissent to European anti-Semitism.

The debate over the Israeli-Palestinian conflict reveals most starkly the dramatic, if not tragic, drifting apart of the United States and Europe, and it testifies to a slow separation of the terms of public debate. Thus, to give an example, in 2002 the chief rabbi in England, Jonathan Sacks,[10] said that many of the things Israel has done to the Palestinians fly in the face of the values of Judaism—"[They] make me feel very uncomfortable as a Jew." He had always believed, he said, that Israel "had to give back all the land [taken in 1967] for the sake of peace." Peaceniks in Israel, such as Amos Oz, take similar views. Even more remarkably, in the wake of the May 2004 rampage by the Israeli Army in the Gaza Strip that left sixteen hundred Palestinians homeless, Justice Minister Tommy Lapid, the only Holocaust survivor in the Israeli government, declared that the house demolitions were inhumane. As the *Guardian Weekly* quoted him: "The demolition of houses in Rafah must stop. It is not humane, not Jewish, and causes us grave damage in the world. At the end of the day, they'll kick us out of the United Nations, try those responsible in the international court in The Hague, and no one will want to speak to us."[11] Many in Europe, Jews and non-Jews alike, would agree. And they have the chance to do so, because Israeli voices such as Lapid's are being aired in the European press. Leading newspapers, in France, in England, in Germany, as well as in other European countries—and let us not forget Israel, with its exemplary *Haaretz* newspaper—do what top-notch journalism is all about: write contemporary history as it unfolds, with all its welcome and unwelcome sides. Good journalists and editorial writers are not loath to say the unwelcome things and confront their readers with all the tragic complexity of life in the Middle East.

Yet it would be hard to hear similar views expressed in the United States, other than in an American equivalent of the Soviet samizdat, or self-publication, which avails itself of the Internet for the spirited exchange of dissenting views. In the public realm, among American Jews, the religious Right, opinion leaders, and Washington political circles, there is a closing of ranks behind the view that everything Israel does to the Palestinians is legitimate self-defense against acts of terrorism. Yet if America's overriding foreign policy concern is the war against terrorism, one element is tragically lacking in its Middle East policy: an attempt to see the United States through the eyes of Arabs, more particularly, Palestinians. A conflation seems to have occurred between the national interests of Israel and the United States, as illustrated by the actions of Richard Perle—foreign policy guru in Washington government circles and a man tellingly of dual Israeli-American citizenship—who did not see any conflict of interest (personal or national) in drafting policy documents for Benjamin Netanyahu's Likud Party in Israel in 1997. The two countries, at the official level, share a definition of the Israeli-Palestinian problems that blinkers them to rival views more openly discussed in Europe.

Among the pieces in *Granta*'s "What We Think of America" issue is one by a Palestinian writer, Raja Shehadeh. He reminded the reader that "today there are more Ramallah people in the U.S. than in Ramallah. Before 1967 that was how most Palestinians related to America—via the good things about the country that they heard from their migrant friends and relations. After 1967, America entered our life in a different way." The author went on to say that the Israeli occupation policy of expropriating Arab land to build Jewish settlements, and roads to connect them, while deploying soldiers to protect settlers, would never have been possible without "American largesse." But American assistance, Shehadeh continued, did not stop at the funding of ideologically motivated programs. In a personal vignette, more telling than any newspaper report, Shehadeh wrote:

Last July my cousin was at a wedding reception in a hotel on the southern outskirts of Ramallah when an F16 fighter jet dropped a hundred-pound bomb on a nearby building. Everything had been quiet. There had not been any warning of an imminent air attack. . . . Something happened to my cousin that evening. . . . He felt he had died and was surprised afterwards to find he was still alive. . . . He did not hate America. He studied there. . . . Yet when I asked him what he thought of the country he indicated that he dismissed it as a lackey of Israel, giving it unlimited assistance and never censoring its use of U.S. weaponry against innocent civilians.

The author concluded with these words: "Most Americans may never know why my cousin turned his back on their country. But in America the parts are larger than the whole. It is still possible that the optimism, energy and opposition of Americans in their diversity may yet turn the tide and make America listen."

The Bush administration, with its preemptive strategy of taking out opponents before they could harm the United States at home or abroad—in much the same way that Israeli fighter jets assassinate alleged Palestinian terrorists, in their cars, homes, and backyards, without bothering about due process or collateral damage—was not likely to create an America that would "listen." Who was not for Bush was against him. Well, so be it. Many Europeans chose not to be bullied into sharing the Bush administration's view of the world. Although they could not command as many divisions as Bush, they surely were able to handle the "divisions" that Bush—the man who, in the 2000 election campaign, portrayed himself as a uniter, not a divider— inflicted on the Atlantic community, if not on Europe itself.

If today there is division between the ways many Europeans "read" the events in the Middle East and the ways many Americans do, it is surely the result of differing exposure to the daily news, which in Europe is presented less selectively, and with less bias. Even several years after President Bush declared the Iraqi mission accomplished, many American reporters in Iraq voluntarily embedded themselves for their own safety in U.S. Marine encampments. As one correspondent, Pamela Constable of the *Washington Post,* described her experience: "I quickly became part of an all-American military microcosm."[12] Michael Massing, in a piece in the *New York Review of Books,* argued that if U.S. news organizations truly wanted to get inside events in Iraq, there was a clear step they could take: incorporate more reporting and footage from international news organizations. Arabic-language TV stations have a wide presence on the ground. European outlets such as the BBC (British Broadcasting Corporation), the *Guardian,* the *Financial Times,* the *Independent,* and *Le Monde* have Arabic-speaking correspondents with close knowledge of the Middle East. Reuters, the Associated Press, and Agence France-Presse have many correspondents stationed in places where U.S. organizations do not. As Massing concluded: "In the current climate, of course, any use of Arab or European material—no matter how thoroughly edited and checked—could elicit charges of liberalism and anti-Americanism. The question for American journalists is whether they really want to know what the Iraqis themselves, in all their complexity, are thinking and feeling."[13] It was a charge against a blinkered and parochial American journalism that is more generally made by Europeans attempting to fathom the depths of the divide between American and European public discourse.[14] A free press, as the highly regarded author and war correspondent Philip Knightley noted in the magazine *Index on Censorship,* would not reduce the post–September 11 debate to "abuse, incitement, personal attacks, inflammatory accusation and intimidation until many a commentator and intellectual, the very people whose voices we want to hear, have been cowed into silence"[15] (or driven underground, we might add, into the American Internet form of samizdat dissent).

But there may also be a deeper force at work. Tellingly, the *Guardian* referred to Tommy Lapid as the sole Holocaust survivor in the current Israeli government. If World War II memories may have resurfaced in Lapid's reading of the Gaza events, something similar may be at work among European audiences. Photographs from Palestine or Iraq may well bring back memories of German retaliatory actions against villages in Europe; they may also bring back remembered photographs of World War II atrocities used powerfully to educate Europeans about the enormity of Nazi rule. They may release a submerged reservoir of remembered images that Europeans do not share with Americans. Yet that basic difference need not drive the two sides of the Atlantic apart. Europeans saw their tragic history repeat itself in the 1990s Balkan wars, but in the end united action under NATO auspices halted the atrocities perpetrated there. Ultimately, Americans and Europeans could both read what had happened as crimes against humanity. Such a shared reading of events in the Middle East and their implications for foreign policy seems to be precisely what is lacking. A widely shared sense of outrage among Europeans, fed by the daily pictures and news reports from the Middle East, translates into impotent anger at an American Middle East policy seen as lacking balance and fairness.

There has been a resurgence of open anti-Americanism in Europe and elsewhere in the world—not least in the Middle East, the area that brought us Osama bin Laden and his paranoid hatred of America and of the West more generally. But if bin Laden can still conflate the two—America *and* the West—why can't we? If Raja Shehadeh still holds hopes of an America that one can make listen, why don't we? Let us face it: we are all Americans, but sometimes it is hard to see the Americans we hold dear in the Americans that hold sway. Those are the dangerous moments when clashing policy views may assume the contours of deeper, more fundamental differences—when difference translates into incompatibility, and the face of just one president may seem to reflect an America that has changed its face more permanently and fundamentally.

What kind of face could that be? As some see it, the United States may have begun to show the effects of long-term cultural trends that increasingly set America apart from Europe. According to the *World Values Survey*, a long-term survey research

project of the University of Michigan, the overall picture is ambivalent.[16] Americans consistently score as high as, or higher
than, Europeans when it comes to values dealing with political
or economic freedoms. Americans and Europeans share ideas
of democracy and freedom and have a common interest in de-
fending those ideas. But the University of Michigan project also
looked at a different set of values and ranked countries along a
conceptual axis ranging from traditionalism to secularism. Traditionalism comprises views that give a central place to religion,
family, and country. At the other end are secular-rational values that emphasize individual choice in matters of lifestyle and
individual emancipation from older frameworks of affiliation
such as the church or the fatherland. Americans' position on that
scale is exceptional among Western countries. Americans lean
much more strongly toward the traditionalist end of the scale
than do Europeans (with the exception of Ireland). Americans
are the most patriotic of Western nations: 72 percent claim to be
"very proud" of their country, thus putting themselves alongside
citizens of such countries as India and Turkey. Americans' position on the religion scale—religion being the single most important gauge of traditionalism according to the survey—puts them
closer to Nigerians and Turks than to Swedes or Germans. And
the differences between the Americans and people from northern and western European countries have, if anything, only in-
creased. Since the first survey, in 1981, Americans have grown
more traditional, Europeans less so. Yet in the other values, those
of democracy and freedom, they have moved in tandem.

From these survey data America appears as a country of a
cultural ambivalence all its own, in an evolving idiosyncratic
symbiosis of traditionalism and modernism. The historical dy-
namics of this symbiosis, with the growing influence of traditionalism, may well have contributed to the mutual alienation
between Europe and the United States. Public discourse on either
side of the Atlantic is losing its shared terms of reference. America's political establishment has long been the safe haven of a

secular, Enlightenment world view that it shared with political elites in Europe. Slowly but surely, however, traditionalism has made inroads into America's centers of policy-making. Of the two main political parties, the Republican Party has targeted its political strategy toward the incorporation of the traditionalist segment among the electorate. The strategy is two-pronged. Contemporary traditionalism has thrived on the ongoing culture war against anything connected to the lifestyle revolution of the 1960s. Its antimodernism may remind us of an earlier high water mark of traditionalism in the 1920s, forever epitomized in the anti-Darwinian Scopes (or "monkey") trial. At the time it may have seemed like traditionalism's last hurrah. Yet with great organizational acumen traditionalism has made a remarkable comeback, waging a cultural war on the forces of moral relativism and libertarianism unleashed in the 1960s. Having gotten its act together politically, it offers itself as a tempting electoral bloc to the Republican Party. Yet the Republican Party is not solely the passive recipient of such support. It has chosen actively to play on the cultural fears of the traditionalists, posturing as the champion of all those who see gay marriage, abortion, divorce, euthanasia, capital punishment, and more such moral issues as defining the political agenda, while casting the Democrats as representing moral depravity. More than ever before in American history, George W. Bush's Republican administration had accommodated the agenda of the religious Right on a wide front, domestically (as in making crucial Supreme Court nominations) or in areas such as creationism and stem cell research, as well as internationally (as in vetoing development programs that include provisions for birth control).

If we can discern two different Americas—one modern and secular, the other centered on traditional values—they seem to coincide with one or the other of the two main parties. America seems to be split down the middle, with its two halves cohabiting in delicate balance. Visiting Europeans, journalists and diplomats among them, cannot fail to notice the widespread alienation from the Bush administration precisely based on a cultural rift as outlined here. This view has become common coinage in press commentaries in *Le Monde* in France, in the *Guardian* in England, and in the *Frankfurter Allegmeine* in Germany, to name just three of the more influential, opinion-forming newspapers in Europe.

Affiliating with the urbane and modern America, as many Europeans are wont to do, they may tend to exaggerate the "moral issues" divide as the single most important determining factor in the Republican Party's electoral strength. Revisiting exit poll and public opinion data, however, the case has been convincingly argued that fear of a different sort may well have ensured Bush's reelection.[17] Against the backdrop of the war on terror, while keeping its ugly face from the general public, cynically manipulating alarm stages, casting Bush as the decisive war leader while painting the opponent as a flip-flopper, the Republican Party employed an electoral strategy that successfully managed to rally behind it all those voting on their fears. There is an Orwellian *1984* quality about this, with ongoing, low-level warfare and scaremongering preparing a population to surrender their democratic freedoms.

The highly partisan nature of such recent trends may remind Europeans that anti-Americanism is not the point. We may believe that we recognize a generic Americanism in any particular American behavior, be it cultural or political. Yet the range of such behavior is simply too wide—ranging in culture from the sublime to the vulgar, and in politics from high-minded internationalism to narrow nationalism—to warrant any across-the-board rejection. Anti-Americanism, if we choose to retain the term at all, should be seen as a weak and ambivalent complex of anti-feelings. It does not apply but selectively, never extending to a total rejection of both forms of Americanism: the cultural and the political. Thus we can have either of two separate outcomes: an anti-Americanism rejecting cultural trends that are seen as typically American, while allowing of admiration for America's energy, innovation, prowess, and optimism; or an anti-Americanism in reverse, rejecting an American political creed that for all its missionary zeal is perceived as imperialist and oppressive, while admiring American culture, from its high-brow to its pop varieties. These opposed directions in the critical thrust of anti-Americanism often go hand in hand with opposed positions on the political spectrum. The cultural anti-Americanism of those rising in defense of Europe's cultural identities is typically on the conservative right wing, whereas the political anti-Americanism of the Cold War and the war in Vietnam typically occurred on the left. Undoubtedly the drastic change in America's position on the world stage since World War II has contributed to this double somersault. Since that war America has appeared in a radically different guise, as much more of a potent force in everyday life in Europe and the larger world than ever before.

As we all know, there is a long history that illustrates Europe's long and abiding affinity with America's daring leap into an age of modernity. It shared America's fascination with the political modernity of republicanism, of democracy and egalitarianism, with the economic modernity of progress in a capitalist vein, and with an existential modernity that saw Man, with a capital M and in the gender-free sense of the word, as the agent of history, the molder of his social life as well as of his own individual identity and destiny. It was after all a Frenchman, Crèvecoeur, who on the eve of American independence pondered the question of "What, then, is the American, this new Man?" A long line of European observers have, in lasting fascination, commented on this American venture, seeing it as a trajectory akin to their own hopes and dreams for Europe.[18] Similarly, French immigrants in the United States, in order to legitimize their claims for ethnic specificity, have always emphasized the historical nexus of French and American political ideals, elevating Lafayette alongside George Washington to equal iconic status.[19]

But as we also know, there is an equally long history of a French, and more generally European, awareness of American culture taking directions that were seen as a threat to European ways of life and views of culture. Whether it was Tocqueville's more sociological intuition of an egalitarian society breeding cultural homogeneity and conformism, or later views that sought the explanation in the economic logic of a free and unfettered market, the fear was of an erosion of the European cultural landscape, of European standards of taste and cultural value. As I have argued elsewhere, the French were not alone in harboring such fears,[20] but they have been more consistently adamant in making the case for a defense of their national identity against a threatening process of Americanization. The very word is a French coinage. It was Baudelaire who, on the occasion of the 1855 Exposition Universelle de Paris, spoke of modern man, set on a course of technical materialism, as "tellement américanisé . . . qu'il a perdu la notion des différences qui caractérisent les phénomènes du monde physique et du monde moral, du naturel et du surnaturel" (. . . as so Americanized as to have lost all sense of the differences setting apart the physical from the moral world, the natural from the supernatural).[21] The Goncourt brothers' *Journal*, from the time of the second exposition in 1867, refers to "L'exposition universelle, le dernier coup à ce qui est l'américanisation de la France" (the Universal Exhibition, the last blow in what is the americanization of France).[22] As these critics saw it, industrial progress ushered in an era in which quantity would replace quality and in which a mass culture feeding on standardization would erode established taste hierarchies. There are echoes of Tocqueville here, yet the eroding factor is no longer the egalitarian logic of mass democracy but the logic of industrial progress. In both cases, however, whatever the precise link and evaluating angle, America had become the metonym for unfettered modernity, like a Prometheus unbound.

These longer lines of anti-Americanism, cultural and political, are alive and well today. And often the two blend into one. Whenever Europeans, particularly young ones dressed in blue jeans and T-shirts, rise in protest against American interventions on the world stage, they go out and smash the windows of a nearby McDonald's (and there is always a McDonald's nearby). As an icon of America's global presence, that fast-food chain represents in the eyes of protesters America's cultural imperialism, but it serves equally well as an emblem of political imperialism. The protest is facile and inarticulate, yet it serves to make a point against American power seen as overbearing and unresponsive. But how about the recent surge of anti-Europeanism in the United States?

Given Europe's daring post–World War II venture in the construction of a European Union, inventing protofederalist forms in the search for a supranational Europe, how do we account for the recent resurgence of anti-Europeanism in the United States? Having promoted and supported this European evolution for many decades, why have so many American opinion leaders now turned anti-European? In the vitriolic vituperation that set the tone of transatlantic exchanges during the Bush years, leading American voices discarded as the "Old Europe" those countries that criticize the drift of American foreign policy, while hailing other countries as the "New Europe" that are willing to follow in America's footsteps. Robert Kagan contributed to this rising anti-Europeanism in the United States when he paraphrased the dictum that men are from Mars, women from Venus. As he chose to present the two poles, Americans now are the new Martians, while Europeans are the new Venutians. Never mind the gendering implied in his view that Europeans are collectively engaged in a feminine endeavor when they pursue the new, transnational, and cosmopolitan Europe. He does make an astute point, though, when he describes the European quest as Kantian, as an endeavor to create a transnational space where laws and civility rule. As Kagan sees it, though, the Europeans are so self-immersed that they are forgetful of a larger world that is Hobbesian, not Kantian, and is a threat to them as much as to the United States. To the extent that Europeans still involve themselves in the larger world, they tend to emphasize peace-keeping operations rather than preemptive military strikes.[23]

Kagan and many others tend to forget that it has taken the United States about a hundred years to find and test its institutional forms and build a nation of Americans from people flooding to its shores from all over the world. It could only have done so while turning its back to the world, in self-chosen isolationism, under the protective umbrella of a Pax Britannica. Europe has had only some forty years to turn its gaze inward when it engaged in shaping the contours of a new Europe. During those years it enjoyed in its turn the protection of an umbrella, provided this time by the Pax Americana. This constellation came to an end along with the Cold War. Yet only then could the European construction fully come into its own, conceiving of the new Europe on the scale of the entire continent. It is a tremendous challenge, and Europe needs time to cope with it. If it succeeds it may well serve as a model to the world, a rival to the American ideal of transnationalism, of constituting a nation of nations. If they are rival models, they are at the same time of one kind. They are variations on larger ideals inspiring the idea of Western civilization, and find their roots in truly European formative moments in history, in the Renaissance, the Reformation, and the Enlightenment. Larry Siedentop places the formative moment even earlier in time, coinciding with the rise of a Christian view of the universal equality of mankind vis-à-vis God. As he presents it, the formative moment consisted in universalizing a religious view that in Judaism was still highly particularist, claiming an exceptionalist relation between God and the people of Israel.[24] This shared heritage inspired the first transatlantic readings of what the terrorist attack of 9/11 signified. It was seen as an onslaught on the core values of a shared civilization. How ironic, if not tragic, then, that before long the United States and Europe parted ways in finding the proper response to the new threat of international terrorism.

As for the United States, the first signs of its farewell to inter-

nationalism in foreign policy—to its Wilsonianism, if you wish—
and to its pioneering role in designing the institutional and legal
framework for peaceful interstate relations in the world, had, as
I pointed out before, actually preceded 9/11. No longer did the
Bush administration conceive of the United States as the primus
inter pares, setting the guidelines for collective action while seeking legitimacy for action through treaties and UN resolutions. As
the one hegemon on the world stage it now felt free to pursue its
national interest through policies that one can only describe as
unilateralist. It might have seemed like a throwback to the time
of nation state sovereignty, a stage of history that Europe is
struggling to transcend. Unspectacular and cumbersome as the
European project may seem, it is already rich in achievement.
It has brought together longtime enemies—like Germany and
France—it has admitted as democratic member states nations
that quite recently knew fascist dictatorships—like Italy, Spain,
and Portugal—or that were under the heel of military dictators
—like Greece. It recently admitted nations that have lived under
communist rule since World War II. Turkey, a longtime member
of NATO and since 1949 a member of the Council of Europe
and subscriber to the European Convention on Human Rights,
is now busy getting its house in democratic order so as to qualify
for membership in the European Union.

Of course, much may go wrong in the further construction of
the European Union. Public opinion, in a hidebound return to
the laagers of national identity and sovereignty, may rally against
future daring steps in the EU's growth and development. Anti-
globalist sentiments may well translate into resentment against
the union's transnational powers. In 2005, in France and the
Netherlands, the project for a European Constitution was voted
down in referenda. But then, the construction of the union so far
has never been neat. It has been a process of muddling through,
of endless compromises between Europe's various national interests. Even so, the power of Europe's promise has touched even
the peoples at its margins. It has redirected their gaze and sense

of national purpose by holding out the hope of eventually join-ing Europe's Kantian space of peace and the rule of law.

If the European project is successful—and as I see it that means the inclusion of Turkey—Europe, I strongly believe, will offer a model to the world, particularly the world of Islam, or for that matter the state of Israel, of a civil and democratic order, multi-national and multicultural, far more tempting than the version of democracy brought under American auspices through preemp-tive military invasion. Those in support of what the United States was pursuing in Iraq blithely called it a neo-Wilsonianism. I beg to differ. If there is a neo-Wilsonian promise, it is held by the new Europe.

In the European repertoire of the cultural critique of America, one observation may have gained in poignancy. Albert Camus and Jean-Paul Sartre in France, or Oswald Spengler in Germany, have been among those who noted an absence in America of the European sense of the tragic. In the blithe meliorism of the American project to bring democracy to the Middle East, what is lacking is the awareness that the active pursuit of good ends may well result in achieving its opposite. As in classic Greek trag-edy, the Gods may strike with blindness those they wish to de-stroy. In the case of America's forward defense of democracy in Iraq, though, the blindness may be self-inflicted, as if its leaders were, and still may be, in a pathological state of denial. When the shocking pictures of systematic humiliation of Iraqi prisoners entered the public realm, President Bush and Secretary Rumsfeld dismissed the acts as un-American. If this is what Americans did, it is not what Americans would do. America is inherently good.[25] Among many others, Romano Prodi, then president of the Eu-ropean Commission in Brussels, begged to differ. Never one to mince words, he affirmed that the Iraq tortures were war crimes, which, for him, made it difficult to see the American presence in Iraq as a peace mission. Others, of a subtler cast of mind, ex-pressed similar views. Thus, in an interview in the *Süddeutsche*

Zeitung on the occasion of his seventy-fifth birthday,[26] German philosopher Jürgen Habermas testified to his disillusionment and disenchantment with the Bush administration and its standard bearers. The experience was all the more painful since, as he acknowledged, he could not have come into his own as a philosopher of public space and democratic debate without the impact of America's pluralist liberalism and its philosophy of pragmatism. Ever since he was sixteen, he said, his political ideas had been nourished by the American enlightenment ideals, thanks to a sensible reeducation policy in the postwar years of American occupation in Germany. But in a 2004 book on the divided West, he had this to say: "Let us not delude ourselves: The normative authority of America lies in shatters."[27] The official manipulation of public opinion and the rampant patriotic conformism he said he would not have deemed possible in the liberal America that he had envisioned.

Let me return to the editor-in-chief of *Le Monde*, Jean-Marie Colombani. Like Habermas, his feelings about the United States have followed a curve from affiliation all the way to alienation, only in a shorter time span. In a May 2004 editorial entitled "Are We All Un-American?"[28] he comments on Rumsfeld's facile dismissal of the Abu Ghraib abominations as un-American. If this implies a definition of true Americanism, it is one that Colombani refuses to share. As Colombani put it: "In the wake of September 11, we all felt ourselves to be Americans. Donald Rumsfeld would make us all un-American." I tend to agree. If the Bush administration showed us the face of a self-righteous, arrogant, and unbridled Americanism, it is an Americanism that I abhor and oppose.

[2]

THE ASCENT OF THE FALLING MAN:
AN ICONIC IMAGE OF 9/11

GIVEN THE RECORD flood of images that in their diverse ways reflect the events of 9/11, there are those who doubt whether any single image is able to stand out from the others through its power to capture the essence of what happened. As one author put it two years after the event: "[T]he enormous swell of image production generated by 9/11 and conflicting ideologies precluded the possibility of any single example holding the field."[1] Looking back, with the benefit of a longer perspective, it seems that a handful of images, in the minds of a larger public, have gained an iconic power that other images lack.

Why is it that some photographs have a power of epic concentration, condensing larger moments in history into one iconic image? The quest for an answer may lead us to reflect on the way the human mind stores arresting moments. Psychologists in their use of the metaphor of "flashbulb memories" suggest an analogy between pictures in the mind—photographs taken by the human eye—and the medium of photography. The power of iconic photographs derives precisely from our feeling that such photographs have done the work of memory for us. They have an impact on the human mind similar to what our eyes would have done, had we been present. They produce the equivalent of "flashbulb memories" for us, turning us into vicarious witnesses, irrespective of distance and time. The effect critically has to do with what one student of the medium has called "the savage silence of photographs."[2] They speak no words, use no rhetorical flourish, no linguistic embellishments or evasions. They are literally before language. They freeze transient motion into lasting stillness. Neither film nor television footage has this power of silence. Stopping time and motion, photography "forcibly fills up our view."[3] Photographs come to us like documents from "the other side," beyond time, beyond life. They are like testaments, last wills drawn up in the service of memory.[4]

The power of photography, thus conceived, is intrinsic to the medium. It does not critically depend on artistry or aesthetics, on an inner vision in the mind of the photographer seeking expression. Iconic photographs, freezing history into memory by making time stand still, have an autonomy of expressive force unconnected to authorial intent or control. This all-perceptiveness of photography, seeing things that would escape the human eye, caused Walter Benjamin to speak of the "unconscious optics" of the medium.[5] The afterlife of iconic photographs is most clearly the area where the photography of history blends into the history of photography. From this perspective photographs most clearly take their place as agents of history, rather than being history's mere reflection. From the moment that photographs acquire iconic status and enter the realm of the mass circulation of images, they begin to affect history rather than merely reflecting it.

Here the closer reading of one particular photograph—*Falling Man* by Richard Drew—may suggest an approach to exploring this power of iconic images. The picture is of a man falling from one of the towers, captured at the fleeting moment when his body seemed to assume the stylized pose of an Olympic diver. As we shall see, the photograph has never been secure in its claim on iconic status. It was contested, even rejected, yet it has managed to endure in an afterlife as the inspiration for some of the finest and most interesting creative responses to the drama and trauma of 9/11.

It is this picture, for example, that provided Don DeLillo with the title for his novel on the tragedy of 9/11. Or in fact more than just the title: the falling man is a haunting presence in the story itself. Drawing on the rich resonance of the falling man as a re-membered iconic image, DeLillo, in an inspired distancing strat-egy, introduces *not* the person so unforgettably caught in midfall by Drew's camera but the enigmatic character of a performance artist, David Janiak, who specializes in reenacting, *not* the fall, but the photographic still; Janiak reenacts the pose of the iconic falling man, hanging upside-down above the pavement, secured to a harness. In DeLillo's words: "There was something awful about the stylized pose, body and limbs, his signature stroke. But the worst of it was the stillness itself."[6] Only much later in the novel is the connection between the photograph and the reenact-ment made explicit. Upon reading an obituary of David Janiak in the newspaper, dead at thirty-nine, apparently of natural causes, the woman protagonist of the novel does an advanced computer search and reads about a dispute over the issue of the posture Janiak assumed during the fall, the posture he maintained in his suspended state. Was this position intended, she reads, to reflect the body posture of a particular man who was photographed falling from the north tower of the World Trade Center, head-first, arms at his sides, one leg bent, a man set forever in free fall against the looming background of the column panels in the tower? "She did not read further but knew at once which photo-graph the account referred to. It hit her hard when she first saw it, the day after, in the newspaper. . . . Headlong, free fall, she thought, and this picture burned a hole in her mind and heart, dear God, he was a falling angel and his beauty was horrific."[7] Thus, almost in passing, DeLillo evokes the afterlife of a single photograph, with its iconic power to burn holes in the minds and hearts of so many.

Falling People, Falling Man

At the time of the attack on New York's Twin Towers many sat in front of their television screens, trying to imagine in anguish and impotence what went on in the towering inferno of the World Trade Center. Yet one response among those trapped in the buildings above the level of impact was clear for all to see. Rather than burn or choke to death people in their hundreds had opted for a death of their own choosing, delivering themselves to the pull of gravity as they jumped from windows on all four sides of the towers. Television images showed many of these individuals until the various channels covering the events stopped broadcasting them. The images were deemed too gruesome, too unmediated a confrontation with the horror of the moment. If the point here was the protection of the public, it may also have been the intention to protect the dignity of the jumpers from the unseemly, if not voyeuristic, intrusion into their utter loneliness, seconds away from death. Although the "jumpers" epitomized most starkly the horror and tragedy of the event, images of their free fall were safely tucked away from the public gaze, preventing their becoming part of a collective memory that would soon be cast in terms of the heroism and bravery of the victims and their saviors. Yet the mental shock and trauma of those who beheld the spectacle of so many people falling, and who will never forget the loud thud of bodies hitting the ground—"it was raining bodies," as one firefighter wailed in shock once he was safely back at his station[8]—does seem to need its own closure through sharing the memory with others.

What is it exactly about images of these individuals falling to their deaths that elicits public reticence? Is it the gulf between the jumpers' experience lasting some thirty seconds and that of a larger public, yearning perhaps to empathize yet prevented from empathy in the case of the falling people? Is it so hard to read a meaning into their fate?

The rich store of photographs and of film and television footage has allowed makers of historical documentaries to return to the images of falling people and carefully to contextualize them. Ric Burns, for example, structures his documentary, *New York: The Center of the World*,[9] as a biblical passion, telling a story that makes it clear to the viewer that the horror of the terrorist onslaught has made for the collective redemption of New Yorkers. Good in the end emerged from evil. Burns has not shrunk for fear of being disrespectful to the dead from showing footage of people leaning out of the upper floors of the two towers, clinging to windowpanes first, then choosing a free fall to certain death. The camera pans from body after body falling down to the stunned faces of the crowd. "My God, Oh, my God," is the continuing litany one hears. There is one voice, though, addressing the cameraman—one must assume—shouting: "You can't take pictures of this." That voice must have spoken on behalf of all those whose gut feeling was one of revulsion against filming this particular aspect of the horror of the World Trade Center attacks.

That feeling must have prevailed in the days following 9/11. The history of Associated Press photographer Richard Drew's photograph testifies to this urge to suppress. Drew had trained his telephoto lens on one man and shot eight frames. Back in his office at the Associated Press, he inserted the disc from his digital camera into his laptop and recognized, instantly, what his camera had seen with its uncanny power to catch, in Benjamin's expression, the "unconscious optics" of human perception. A moment no observer's eye could have consciously noticed was forever frozen in a frame. In a split-second moment all the visual ingredients that went into the picture had, as if in a kaleidoscope, assumed a transient configuration that seemed to suggest a transcendent reading. Drew did not even look at any of the other pictures in the sequence. He didn't have to. "You learn in photo editing to look for the frame," he says. "You have to recognize it. That picture just jumped off the screen because of its verticality and symmetry."[10] The next morning the photograph appeared on page seven of the *New York Times* and in a number of other newspapers across the country. Yet, as Richard Drew remembers it, "Most newspapers refused to print it. Those who did, on the day after the World Trade Center attacks, received hundreds of letters of complaint. The photograph was denounced as cold-blooded, ghoulish and sadistic. Then it vanished."[11]

Drew had photographed dying before. As a twenty-one-year-old rookie photographer on a supposedly routine assignment, he was standing behind Robert F. Kennedy when he was assassinated. He was so close that Kennedy's blood spattered onto his jacket. He kept taking photographs, even when a distressed Ethel Kennedy tried to fend off Drew and his intrusive camera eye. Nobody at the time refused to print those photographs. They became iconic images and established Drew's fame. What then is it about Drew's image of the falling man that people initially found so offensive?

As Tom Junod describes the photograph in a piece for *Esquire* magazine, it differs from *all* other photographs of people falling from the Twin Towers. All the other images show people who appear to be struggling against horrific discrepancies of scale. They are made puny by the backdrop of the towers, which loom like colossi, and then by the event itself. They flail, twist, and turn, their shoes fly off. There is no semblance of control. The man in Drew's iconic picture, by contrast, is perfectly vertical, head down, seemingly poised and in full control of his posture. The image shows him in perfect accord with the lines of the buildings behind him. He splits them, bisects them. Everything to the left of him in the picture is the North Tower; everything to the right, the South Tower. Junod goes on to say, movingly and perceptively: "Though oblivious to the geometric balance he has achieved, he is the essential element in the creation of a new flag, a banner composed entirely of steel bars shining in the sun. Some people who look at the picture see stoicism, willpower, a portrait of resignation; others see something else—something discordant and therefore terrible: freedom."[12] The man does not appear intimidated by gravity's lethal force, rather seems to defy it. His arms are by his side. His left leg is bent at the knee, almost casually. He offers the ultimate image of grace in the face of death. Yet only seconds before or after, like the others who had jumped, he had flailed, twisted, and turned. No human eye could have caught this moment of transcendence and stillness, a moment frozen forever. The power of this one image, so richly suggestive of redemptory readings, is quintessentially photographic.

To those who are willing to set aside their sense of disrespectful intrusion, this detached reading of the photograph suggests all the elements that make for an iconic photograph. In its suggestion of grandeur and grace, in its intertextual evocation of Jasper Johns's many variations on the theme of the American flag, in the "savage silence" of a man stopped in mid-fall forever, it would appear to offer, in epic concentration, an emblem of grandeur and humility that would far transcend the sound and fury of 9/11. It would seem to make it the perfect American icon for Americans at a time of national sorrow.

But there are those who may never summon such Olympian detachment nor see the redemptive power of the picture of the falling man, leaving the picture to speak for itself. There have been attempts at establishing the identity of the man in the photograph.[13] Different trails led to potential relatives and may give us a clue to the diverse ways in which people interpret the act of jumping to a death of one's own choosing. One trail led to a Catholic immigrant family from Latin America, the Hernandezes, another to a woman from Connecticut. The Hernandez family, when confronted with the photograph, refused to accept that the photograph might show their husband and father, who had been a restaurant worker at the top floor of the World Trade Center. As they saw it, he would never have jumped. They looked at the decision to jump as a betrayal of love, an unconscionable suicide that went against everything their Catholic faith taught them. The woman in Connecticut had lost two sons in the terrorist attack, both working on the equity desk of an investment firm in the Twin Towers. From a Protestant background, she looked at the decision to jump as a loss of hope—as an absence that we, the living, now have to live with. She chose to live with it, not by angrily rejecting the picture, but by confronting it, by trying to know—by making an act of private witness. Yet a third trail led to the family of an African American preacher from Mount Vernon, New York. The man in the picture may have been Jonathan Briley, the preacher's son. The strong Baptist worldview of the family seems to have inspired them to see the falling man in a different light. As his sister Gwendolyn ruminated, "I never thought of the falling man as Jonathan, I thought of him as a man that just took his life in his hands for just a second. Did that person have so much faith that he knew that God would catch him or was he afraid to experience the end up there? I hope we're not trying to figure out who he is and more to figure out who we are through watching it."[14] These are words that perfectly capture the redemptive reading of Drew's iconic photograph. They suggest more strongly than I have done that the lasting suspension of the falling man may be seen as an act of God, rather than a quirk of photography.

These responses may suggest a more general clue to the widely varied ways in which Americans and others have coped with images of people jumping to their deaths from the Twin Towers. I know of no research data to confirm the following speculation. Yet, on the Internet, long lists can be found of statements by individuals, paying homage to whoever they think the jumper may have been, Norberto Hernandez or Jonathan Briley.[15] The attempts at identifying the lone jumper in Drew's picture may serve many people to cope with the enormity of so many unidentified, anonymous persons choosing to jump and fall to their deaths. It may help them to sympathize and extend the redemptive quality in Drew's image to all these single desperate acts. A more general issue to be raised here, though, is that the effort at identifying the falling man misses the point of the picture's iconicity. (In the case of the Napalm Girl in Nick Ut's iconic Vietnam photograph, the fact that her identity is now known has not detracted from the power of the image.) Drew's Falling Man will live on, I am sure, as the photographic equivalent of the Unknown Soldier, as a photographic *lieu de mémoire* inviting reflections on the history of 9/11 and its meanings.

The likelihood of the image definitely attaining such full iconic status, of its finding its place in the continued quest for the meaning of 9/11, may be confirmed by the history of its afterlife. It has already inspired creative work by other artists. Don DeLillo took his creative cue from this specific photograph, not from the generalized imagery of jumpers. (It is easy to miss this point and not pay due respect to individual photographs. For example, Jonathan Safran Foer's 9/11 novel, *Extremely Loud and Incredibly Close*, for its final flip-through pages uses a photograph by Lyle Owerko, *not* as is often stated, Drew's image.)[16]

Struggling to come up with the proper language, the proper metaphors, for understanding what the collapse of the Twin Towers may have signified, those reflecting on the meaning of Ground Zero may well come to construct their narratives around the central metaphor of the fall, in all its rich, intertextual resonance. In a perceptive essay, Devin Zuber, like Walter Benjamin's Paris flaneur transposed to New York, reflects on the changed reading of one of the largest and most unknown public sculptures in lower Manhattan, several blocks north of the World Trade Center, Roy Shifrin's *Icarus*. The sculpture depicts Icarus at the very end of the Greek legend. The torso is headless and wingless, tilted at such an angle as to suggest not Icarus's winged ascension, his hubris before the fall, but the fall itself. The sculpture was positioned in such a way that the form was perfectly juxtaposed against the looming bulk of the Trade Center towers. At night one had the perspective of the statue falling down the dark space between the two towers. Only now can the sculpture assume its full mythological power as an emblem of human hubris "before the fall."[17]

If the statue can be seen to prefigure 9/11, Art Spiegelman, in

his *In the Shadow of No Towers*, after the fact creatively recon-
figures the imagery and meaning of falling from the sky.[18] Once
again using the medium of the comic book, or graphic novel, that
he had used before in *Maus* as a distancing ploy to describe the
formation of his "postmemory" of the Holocaust,[19] Spiegelman
now tries to control the traumatic impact of the events of 9/11.
Plate #6 of *In the Shadow of No Towers* shows on the left-hand
side a full-length image of the tower in the last moments before
its collapse. A man is seen jumping from it, preferring the freedom of the sky above death by fire, fantasizing, as the text has
it, about "a graceful Olympic dive as his last living act." The
author then adds these amazing words: he is "haunted now by
the images he didn't witness." What turned him into a secondary
witness of 9/11, what formed his postmemory of the events, were
not stories told to him as in the case of *Maus* but may well have
been Drew's image of what truly was a graceful Olympic dive.[20]
Thus, in his own creative way, Spiegelman too illustrates the
way in which a person's repertoire of memories may have been
formed while undergoing the force of Drew's iconic photograph.

In conclusion, let me emphasize that what is important, is not
the making of a final selection of just one, ultimate iconic representation of 9/11 in a single image. There are those to whose
minds 9/11 as a day of infamy will bring remembered images of
towers ablaze, of people running for safety, of two monuments
of the New York skyline collapsing. They are all, in their own
right, images of 9/11 as spectacle, leaving the spectator in the
role of impotent, outside observer. My focus has been on those
harrowing pictures of victims, of people jumping from the towers toward a death of their own choosing. They are pictures that
make for painful empathy with their fate. And this is why they
will continue to resonate in the public memory. Within that body
of photographs of falling people, my point has been to account
for the impact that one image in particular, Drew's "Falling
Man," has had on so many viewers. My purpose has been to
account for the fascination of that one image, in a struggle to

find words to describe that impact. To that end I looked at how others—the photographer himself, Tom Junod, Don DeLillo, Art Spiegelman—have translated their fascination into language that may help us account for the way this image continues to haunt us.

[3]

COOL HAND LUCK: HOW AMERICA PLAYED
ITS HAND ENTERTAINING THE WORLD

FOLLOWING THE ESTABLISHING shots of a bombed-out Berlin in Billy Wilder's classic film *A Foreign Affair* (1948), there is a telling vignette of life resuming its course amid the ruins of the city. It is a scene of a street market near the Brandenburg Gate, where goods change hands in what is basically a barter economy. At one point we see a Soviet soldier looking for a new wristwatch. The display counter, it turns out, are the arms of an American soldier. They are covered with watches that are revealed one by one as the American pulls up his sleeves. The Soviet customer is hard to please, until, at one point, his face lights up, and he shouts in joyful recognition: "Mickey Mouse, Mickey Mouse!" The watch with the face of Walt Disney's emblematic mouse has a new owner while triggering a store of happy childhood memories. The long slog of war all the way from the Russian heartland to Berlin has found its reward.

What are we to make of this fleeting moment? Wilder, with a delightfully light touch of cynicism, offers a morality play of naive, high-minded American idealism facing the reality check of life in a city where the dictates of survival make light of moral standards. In his brief cameo appearance, Mickey Mouse reminds us of some of the hidden strengths in the American arsenal of domination. Americans in the early years of their occupation policies were groping for guidelines, feeling their way around in the uncharted terrain of foreign affairs. While engaging in the dirty compromises of "having a foreign affair," unwittingly replaying Jamesian encounters between American innocence and the wicked ways of Europe, they brought their own repertoires of seduction to bear.

Of course, in the early postwar years Mickey Mouse was just one among those disjointed snippets of American mass culture that had scattered across the globe in the first half of the century. They had not yet congealed into one coherent mass-cultural flood that would irresistibly wash across the globe, offering a consistent reading of "America" as an imaginary construct, the emblem of a country and a culture holding forth a vision of the "good life," of an empire of consumption, or rather the emporium of a democracy of goods available to all. There was an implied message of democracy here, in the sense of a democracy of goods and pleasures, accessible to all and deeply affecting the sense of citizenship as an entitlement to consumerist participation.[1] In a process evolving over the postwar years, in all countries of Western Europe, the various disjointed snippets of a pleasurable American mass culture would undergo a semiotic shift, resulting in a perception of the various snippets as so many ingredients jointly constituting this larger enticing America. In a Europe of postwar scarcity America came to represent this tempting image of a plethora of goods. It did this through Hollywood movies, through the Marshall Plan, through advertising in the illustrated press—in other words, through a combination of commerce and cultural diplomacy. In the process "America" acquired its tempting aura. It turned into a brand, adding its seductive appeal to the separate items of consumption the United States exported. Thus a repertoire developed of American consumption goods, from blue jeans to kitchens, from cigarettes to cars, from films to music, vying for market share while crucially and at the same time performing an informal function of cultural diplomacy. They were all turned into cultural ambassadors evoking American dreams in the minds of foreign publics.

Mickey Mouse early on illustrated this cultural offensive. He could avail himself of all the mastery of American mass-cultural production and dissemination. Not only had he managed to create eager consumers in the United States and elsewhere, enjoying his antics in print and on screen, he also blithely underwent a process of merchandising, linking his appeal to consumer products such as wristwatches. The vignette in Billy Wilder's film illustrates this conjunction. It also illustrates the process through which America's popular cult figures ride piggybacking through the world, establishing semiotic outposts that would increasingly turn into bridgeheads for an imaginary America. It is a process of cultural conquest under the aegis of commercial market inroads. While gaining access to foreign markets, America's products doubled as agents of cultural penetration.

Two examples may suffice to make this more general point. They take us ahead in time to the post–Cold War era, right into the heart of former Soviet domain. While bordering on the space of a European Union casting about for meaningful emblems to signify its appeal to the populations of the former Soviet Union, icons of American popular culture, with all their semiotic radiance, had vaulted effortlessly across Europe to land ostentatiously in the midst of Eastern European space. Two photographs, taken in the Crimea in the late 1990s, testify to this cultural invasion. One graphically shows the confrontation between an emblem of the ancien régime, a statue of Lenin grimly sizing up the challenge posed by the golden arches of McDonald's. The other shows the presence of the Marlboro Man, Mr. Cool himself, in the characteristic repose of a Westerner who for a change has ventured east. If, in addition to his appeal to cigarette smokers, he tells a taller story, it is one—so to speak—of "How *the East* Was Won" (to paraphrase the title of an iconic 1962 Hollywood Western).

Both photographs are from the time when the semiotic shift that I mentioned had already taken place, when the individual

Lenin Meets McDonald's, Crimea, 2001. *Monique van Hoogstraten, Private Collection.*

bits of American popular culture had already found their place in the larger iconography of an imaginary America. Not only had McDonald's hamburgers and Marlboro cigarettes pried open markets for themselves, they had also irresistibly made way for the Americanization of popular tastes and individual dreams. They offered iconic heroes for people to identify with and to style their identities as their own free agents. Or at least such is the promise held out by American popular culture.

Of course this is a story that keeps repeating itself and has been the stuff of much study focusing on the general theme of the Americanization of the world. Had Jean-Paul Sartre been alive and seen the Marlboro Man in the Crimea, he would have been reminded of his brief infatuation with Western heroes that he had seen in Hollywood Westerns, as "Men of unreflective action," "men who thought little, spoke little and always did the right thing," men that to Sartre appeared like the prototype of the existentialist man, the embodiment of his existentialist ideas.[2] He

The Marlboro
Man in the Crimea,
2001. *Monique van
Hoogstraten, Private
Collection.*

might have labeled them "cool," had he been aware of the term.
It was an image that must have come to Sartre while he watched
Hollywood films, one of the powerful transmitters of American
heroes and cultural icons. Sartre's infatuation did not last. His
critical left-wing views turned him away from admiring adoption of American cultural repertoires to a critical deconstruction
of America as an imperialist power. The lure of Americanization
was fended off by his later vehement anti-Americanism, cultural
and political. His was an intellectual trajectory traveled by many
intellectuals in Europe and elsewhere.

In Europe's lasting encounter with American mass culture,
many were the voices expressing a concern about its negative
impact. Cultural guardians in Europe saw European standards
of taste and cultural appreciation eroded by an American way
with culture that aimed at a mass market, elevating the lowest
common denominator of mass preferences to the main vector of
cultural production. This history of cultural anti-Americanism

in Europe has a long pedigree. In its earlier manifestations, crucially in the years following World War I, the critique of American mass culture was highly explicit, and had to be. Many ominous trends of an evolving mass culture in Europe had to be shown to have originated in America, reaching Europe under clear American agency. An intellectual repertoire of Americanism and Americanization evolved in a continuing attempt at cultural resistance against the lures of a culture of consumption. Never mind that such cultural forms might have come to Europe autonomously, even in the absence of an American model. America served to give a name and a face to forces of cultural change that would otherwise have been anonymous and seemingly beyond control.[3]

Recent Trends: America as a Subtext

Today this European repertoire is alive and kicking. Yet, ironically, as a repertoire that has become common currency to the point of being an intellectual stereotype rather than an informed opinion, America nowadays is often a subtext, unspoken in European forms of cultural resistance. One example may serve to illustrate this. A political poster for the Socialist Party in Salzburg, in the run-up to municipal elections in the city, shows us the determined face and the clenched fist of the party's candidate. He asks the voting public whether the younger generation would not be losers, and called on the electorate to "fight, fight, and fight." What for? "In order to avoid that young people would get fed up with the future." ("Damit unsere Jugend die Zukunft nicht satt hat.") In a visual pun, at the poster's dead center, the getting fed up is illustrated by the blurred image of a hamburger flying by at high speed. Fast food indeed. The call for action is now clear. Austrians should try to fend off a future cast in an American vein. To make this point, American culture is condensed into the single image of the hamburger. It is enough to trigger the larger repertoire of cultural anti-Americanism.

Election poster, Salzburg. *Photograph by the author.*

We may choose to see this poster as only a recent version of cultural guardianship that has always looked at the younger generation as a stalking horse, if not a Trojan horse, for American culture. In fact, historically, it has always been younger generations who, in rebellion against parental authority and cultural imposition, opted for the liberating potential of American mass culture. Yet interesting changes may have occurred in this pattern. Today young people as well, in their concern about forces of globalization, may target the United States as the central agency behind these global trends. They may smash the windows of a nearby McDonald's or may choose more creative and subtle forms of protest. Yet again America tends to be the unspoken subtext in their resistance against global cultural icons.

One more example may serve to illustrate this point. Let me draw on a music video, "Big Beñat," by a Basque group, "Fermin Muguruza," released in the late 1990s. The video, in its own right, is an act of cultural emancipation. The lyrics are in the Basque language, and the station broadcasting the video has all-Basque programming. This may suggest localism, if not cultural provincialism. Nothing would be further from the truth. What we have here is a perfect example of "glocalisation," Roland Robertson's neologism for the interplay between globalization and localization. The music used, Ska, is a staple of "world music," hailing from the Caribbean and popularized through the British music industry. The format of the music video itself is part of global musical entertainment. Yet the message is local. What the video shows is a confusing blend of the traditional and the modern. The opening shot shows a man using a scythe to cut grass. The camera moves up and shows a modern, international-style office block. A mobile phone rings, and the grass-cutter answers the call. More images show modern life. We see an old man talking into a microphone strapped to his head, as if he is talking to himself. We see a group of young men working out in tandem on a flat-back truck driven through the streets, like a transported glimpse of an American gym, with barcodes on their close-cropped heads, suggestive of their being no more than interchangeable, homogenized parts of a larger machine, yet in complete isolation. Then the protagonists of the video appear, with a rickety van, getting ready to sell the local variety of Basque fast food, a sausage on a roll. The very smell breaks the isolation of people caught in the alienating life of modernity. They all flock to the sausage stand to get a taste of true Basqueness. They come to life, spurred by an alleged authenticity of traditional Basque life. The lyrics of the chorus repeat: "Down with McDonald's, Long live Big Beñat!" (the name of the Basque delicacy).

The claim made in this video is in behalf of the authenticity of regional cultures struggling to survive in a world threatened by the homogenizing forces of globalization. Yet the medium of communication testifies to the impact of precisely those forces as much as it protests against them.[4] There is much irony in all this, but most important is the fact that what is shown as modernity truly revives a long repertoire of European cultural anti-Americanism. America *is* modernity, and the long history of European resistance to America is truly a story of resisting the onslaught of modernity on Europe's checkered map of regional and/or national cultures. The terms of resistance are defined by the fact that cultural resistance today takes place in a context that, though increasingly global, still falls under the hegemonic sway of an American culture gone global. If this is the outcome of a long process, let us now turn to the question of origins, of how America's cultural sway has come about, or rather how America has managed to establish itself as a cultural empire.

America's Cultural Empire

The word "empire" is richly suggestive. It calls forth in our minds images of a vast geographic expanse, coinciding with a reach of political and military control extending from one clear center to far-flung frontiers, usually contested. If these are the geopolitical associations we tend to connect with the word, it has different connotations as well. As any good dictionary will remind us, it is possible to "hold empire," as in the expression "to hold empire over the minds of men." This then is to do with the psychological, or cultural, dimension of empire.

When the topic is America, and the question to be answered is whether America, or more precisely, the United States, can be seen as an empire, the challenge is to place the country generically as an empire among empires, while at the same time acknowledging the specifics of the case. After all, America is a late joiner, an imperial upstart. It came to its imperial position under conditions radically different than previous empires had known. Much as it found inspiration in its early days as a republic in the history of Rome and Athens, once it consolidated its existence as a continental state it saw itself carried forward by the great modernizing transformations of the time: in industrial production, in communication, in technological know-how, and in political democracy. In the language of the day Americans saw themselves engaged in the pursuit of their manifest destiny, and, tellingly, of the westward course of empire. It was their way of placing themselves in teleological traditions dating back to Virgil and Bishop Berkeley, yet at the same time they invented novel ways of pursuing ancient dreams. They could act in a world, from the late nineteenth century on, that went through the early stages of globalization, making for a geopolitical theater of shrinking distances and increasing connectivity and interdependence. All these trends would pick up speed during what would become known as "the American century." And with reason. America, as a relatively new actor on the world stage, came to be seen as the center of modernity, a new center of gravity toward which the political compasses across the globe came to point. In the course of the twentieth century it evolved into the hub of networks in global communication, in finance, in production and innovation, in military technology, and in the techniques of mass entertainment. In the pursuit of its manifest destiny it availed itself of all these transformations, more successfully than any rival.

Thus, as it emerged triumphantly from World War II, it quickly consolidated its hegemonic sway by brilliantly interweaving the various strands of imperial reach, benefiting from the many feedback loops that modernity provided. It could turn itself into the "irresistible empire," as Victoria de Grazia felicitously calls it, by mercurially morphing from one tempting model of modernity into another. Thus, as the obvious military hegemon in post–World War II days, it could use its power to give guidance to the political and economic restructuring of Europe through the Marshall Plan, facilitating trade and reconstruction through economic assistance. It also used its power to pry open European markets for America's mass cultural products, foremost among them Hollywood's film production. Film in particular was not just a commodity subject to the logic of free trade but also a tool of cultural diplomacy, exposing European publics to the seductive power of America's dream worlds, of fantasies of the good life as conceived by Americans. Thus America proved expert at turning the hard power of its dominance, military and economic, into the soft power of holding empire over the minds of men, shaping their cultural appetites and dreams in ways that have led observers to speak of Americanization.

Interwoven as the forms of America's dominance are, interconnected as the ways may be in which America holds empire, in the following I propose to disentangle two dimensions, one cultural, to do with the process of Americanization, the other to do with the hard power involved in holding empire. Each part of my argument revolves around a central dilemma. In the case of America's cultural empire the dilemma is one of agency on the part of those subject to the process of Americanization: what precisely is the freedom of choice when people style their lives after American models? This particular constellation of the ways in which America holds empire points up the specifically modern, if not postmodern, form of its hegemonic power. It suggests a voluntary subordination of those under the sway of America's imperial reach that has led some observers to speak of empire by invitation, or empire by adoption. Yet this is only part of the story. Repeatedly, America has had to rely on classic forms of hard power to retain imperial control, fighting wars and sending armies to the far corners of empire. These uses of hard power, I would argue, take us to the consideration of the central dilemma that resides in the tenuous symbiosis between the hard power sustaining empire and the survival of democracy. This dilemma will engage us in our further exploration of the dimensions of anti-Americanism. Often the resistance to America's exercise of hard power, as at the time of the Vietnam War, its armed intervention in the Balkan wars of the 1990s, or later on its invasion of Iraq, produced strange fusions of American cultural icons and its hard-power exploits. Antiwar protesters at the time of the Vietnam War often went clad in blue jeans and T-shirts, sporting the effigies of America's countercultural heroes, like Angela Davis. On the other hand, as we mentioned before, protest could take its aim at mass-cultural icons such as McDonald's. In almost a dance of musical chairs, America's soft-power emblems could change places with the symbols of their hard-power presence in the world, its embassies, its military bases. But let us try to disentangle the two and first look more closely at American empire as resting on its uses of soft power.

Journalist Ron Suskind, who at the time worked for the *New York Times,* has this telling story about an exchange with a White House aide, possibly Karl Rove himself, presidential advisor to George W. Bush:

> The aide said that guys like me [journalists like Suskind] were "in what we call the reality-based community," which he defined as people who "believe that solutions emerge from your judicious study of discernible reality." . . . "That's not the way the world really works anymore," he continued. "We're an empire now, and when we act, we create our own reality. And while you're studying that reality—judiciously, as you will—we'll act again, creating other new realities, which you can study too, and that's how things will sort out. We're history's actors . . . and you, all of you, will be left to just study what we do."[5]

This is a far cry indeed from a Jeffersonian "empire of liberty," let alone an "empire of reason."[6] What Suskind was offered was a view of a postmodern, deconstructionist world in which the reality principle no longer set any meaningful constraints—a view not of an empire of reason, but of a realm where human volition, like a Nietzschean "will to power," was in command. "We are an empire now, and when we act, we create our own reality." This voluntarist, if not cavalier, attitude toward truth and reality may remind one of the famous line by the newspaper man in John Ford's *The Man Who Shot Liberty Valance* (1962): "This is the West, Sir. When the legend becomes fact, we print the legend."

The words quoted by Suskind may strike us like the musings of a delusional mind, more likely to be encountered behind the walls of an asylum than inside the White House. They evoke an "Alice in Wonderland" world, where you can put a president, dressed in bomber jacket, on an aircraft carrier under a banner declaring "Mission Accomplished" and present that as a reality newly created. They are words conveying a megalomania that in the 1960s Senator J. William Fulbright had already diagnosed as the "arrogance of power."[7] But at the same time they are shrewd words, even words of wisdom. They point to what has driven imperial projects throughout history, in a quest for domain and dominance. Time and time again new realities *have* been created and space been opened up for hegemony to be established and an imperial writ to run. Not every attempt along such lines need end in parody, in a object lesson in human hubris. As a long line of studies of empire have shown, there is an arch to the history of empires, a rise followed by decline, but their natural histories, their life cycles, constitute a substantive body of historical reality, more than being the elusive chimeras conjured before our eyes by the illusionism of our postmodern culture of mediated spectacle. There are substantive realities calling for scholarly attention, although they may be hidden from view by their rendition as media spectacle. We may see this illustrated in the "shock and awe" media version of the invasion of Iraq in 2003, or of the television rendition of the first Gulf War as a high-tech spectacle. In response, French semiotician Jean Baudrillard felt induced to write on the alienating experience of watching history unfold on the TV screen. He ironically titled his little book: *The Gulf War Did Not Take Place* (1991).

When Baudrillard chooses to focus on the illusionism and media manipulation attending the display of imperial power, when he highlights the reduction of a real war being waged to the entertainment value of a video war game, he reminds us of the reality principle in history, and of its real cost in human lives and human suffering. Yet at the same time he reminds us of what we might call the principle of *virtual* reality in our postmodern world, where mass audiences live by the very fictions conjured before their eyes. Virtual worlds and virtual realities are the permanent setting of many people's contemporary lives. An astute observer of this is German film maker Wim Wenders. Fascinated from an early age by America and American culture, yet increasingly aware of the Americanization of the culture of his German homeland, he had one character in his film *Kings of the Road* come up with this aphorism: "The Yanks have colonized our subconscious." This one line beautifully captures a central dimension of the sway that America holds over people's imaginations, inside and beyond its national borders. It is the power of what is commonly referred to as America's cultural imperialism, yet a power that gainsays anything the word "imperialism" suggests. American cultural conquest works through the subconscious of its subjects, colonizing it almost by stealth, shaping people's cultural appetites, tastes, yearnings, and needs in an American vein simply by exposing them to its radiance and appeal.

Of course, all empires have used entertainment to keep the populace contented, famously through "bread and circuses," as the Romans had it, but they were not like anything we find in present-day mass media of communication and entertainment. Mass culture has undergone a modernizing transformation, in all its stages from production, through its dissemination and advertising, to its eventual consumption. And American mass culture, from its early formation in the late nineteenth century to the present day, has always managed to corner the world market and expose a world audience to its impact.[8]

Studying this impact, scholars of Americanization have pointed to the pleasure principle in the reception of American mass culture. In its many forms, American mass culture offered a free range for the imagination to roam, allowing people to consider alternative lifestyles and identities, suggesting a freedom to be your own agent in projecting your life. Yet, as critics of mass culture have pointed out all along, there was always the threat of enslavement, of mass culture offering nothing more than an opiate for the people. This line of critique has evolved from being a cheap form of vulgar Marxism into a rather subtle form of deconstructionism, in tune with the "linguistic turn" taken by the new American Studies.[9] This recent trend has led many Americanists to revisit the very language they use and critically to examine the tacit assumptions underlying the concepts central to their understanding of America. As recent presidential addresses to the American Studies Association (ASA) illustrate, this self-examination can go so far as to lead to a call for deleting the word "America" from American Studies, as a concept inherently indoctrinating and imperialist (cf. Radway). Key words in traditional American Studies are seen as tools of indoctrination by stealth, inducing a world view subject to American agency and control. This is probably what Wim Wenders had in mind when he spoke of America colonizing the Europeans' sub-conscious. What the new American Studies approach pursues is to uncover the way this process works and to point to language as the Trojan horse smuggling in covert readings and meanings, presenting them as conventional and natural while subtly bending and subverting people's views of the world.

It is an approach that in spite of its claims of novelty is reminiscent of good old-fashioned Marxist *Ideologiekritik*, bringing tacit ideological structures to light through critical analysis. From that more general perspective it appears that there are longer lines of self-reflexive critical writing in American Studies, particularly so in American Studies varieties inspired by cultural studies sensibilities. Be that as it may, it is certainly the case that the serious study of American mass culture, as one of the tools allowing the United States to hold empire over the minds of others, needs the double focus. We need to understand why people outside America's borders, as well as inside, willingly let themselves be drawn into a universe of American invention, doing so of their own free will. Using the other focus, we also need to understand what hidden messages they expose themselves to while enjoying the fun. That is the part where American agency comes into play, the agency of the sender rather than the receiver. And not only do Americanists need to do this for our present day and age, they need to go back in time and trace the longer history of ideological manipulation (or of attempted mind control) exerted through the dissemination of American mass culture.

A good case in point is another presidential address to the ASA, Amy Kaplan's 2003 discussion of "Violent Belongings and the Question of Empire."[10] She notes that the word "empire" has entered general discussion in the United States on a scale not seen before. Instead of being an empire in denial, or an empire that does not dare speak its name, it is fashionable now, Kaplan says, to debate whether this is a new imperialism or business as usual, whether the United States should be properly called imperial or hegemonic, whether it is benevolent or self-interested, whether it should rely on hard power or soft power, whether this empire most closely resembles the British empire or the Roman, and whether it is in ascendency or decline.[11] She goes on to make this important point: "I am not interested in joining these debates here but in discussing the language that frames them and how the word *empire* appears in a constellation of other words in the political lexicon, such as *terrorism* and *homeland*."[12] The denial and disavowal of empire, she goes on to argue, has long served as the ideological cornerstone of U.S. imperialism and a key component of American exceptionalism. She describes her own approach as a method of exposure, one that reveals the repressed violence embedded in cultural productions or that recovers stories of violent oppression absent from prior master historical narratives.

These words precisely describe the program for a new American Studies as it has evolved in recent years, a program that aims at unveiling the techniques that mass-cultural productions avail themselves of in communicating imperial readings of the world, seen from an American vantage point. Much work in this vein, by Kaplan herself and many others, has looked at the ways in which early forms of American mass culture—the "yellow press," World's Fairs, Wild West shows, early film rushes of the storming of San Juan Hill (mostly studio reenactments, by the way)—entertained the masses while at the same time communicating the exhilaration of imperial ventures and the psychological satisfactions of forming the top tier of hierarchies of race and civilization. Many of these readings were subliminal and unreflective, insinuating themselves into the "normal" ways of conceiving of the world.

Yet at the same time many of these readings were a conscious part of the cultural productions of the late nineteenth century, put there by cultural entrepreneurs who as a group represented the cultural elite of the time. They were engaged in establishing and sustaining the forms of cultural hegemony and cultural capital that Antonio Gramsci and later on Pierre Bourdieu have theorized. Earlier historical research has looked at the elite levels in society, at the circles in politics, journalism, and intellectual life, that gave articulate support to America's imperialist stance.[13] Such support could come from unexpected corners, including prominently the Progressives of the time. While being critical of big business at home for excessive profits and substandard wages, they saw nothing incongruous when they also supported American investments abroad in the interest of expanded markets. The man most convincingly articulating this spirit of the time was Herbert Croly in his *The Promise of American Life*. As Croly argued, Theodore Roosevelt's imperial ventures were an important phase of the new religion of national reform, steps toward the fulfillment of the promise of American life. There were only a few dissenters among American Progressives, such as Jane Addams, but most shared fully in cherishing the aspirations of middle-class America, including the new sense of delight in the rise of the United States as a world power. There was a new, more modern and activist, sense of the national interest that appealed to Roosevelt. It was to inspire Roosevelt's Osawatomie address and lead to his break with the conservative Old Guard. Historical research in this vein allows us to explore the reigning views held by America's elites as they were vying for cultural hegemony. It helps us to focus on the forms of public discourse used at the time to express such reigning views.

Yet, at the same time, at a more popular level these visions and enthusiasms would inform cultural productions intended for mass consumption. Cultural historians and Americanists of a more recent vintage are adding to our understanding of how such hegemonic views could end up holding empire over the minds of Americans first, and of foreign audiences later on, following their exposure to America's mass culture. America's mastery of forms of mass entertainment, coming to full fruition in the latter half of the nineteenth century, aimed first at Americanizing the millions of strangers in its midst, the hordes of immigrants coming to its shores. Having mastered the trick of conveying its readings of America as a meaningful construct across the manifold cultural lines dividing its heterogeneous population, it could then avail itself of this cultural competence in exposing foreign publics to its cultural programs. As it turned out, America proved equally successful in crossing the many national divides that had cordoned off national cultures before. It entertained the many, while exposing them to implied readings of America's sway, cultural and political as well. Mickey Mouse may have been an early trail blazer, bringing happiness and joy wherever he went. But as we have seen, sometimes a mouse is more than a mouse, an insidious rodent patiently gnawing away at the foundations of cultural sovereignty abroad.

MUSICAL AMERICA: STAGING THE U.S.A.
TO THE SOUNDS OF MUSIC

WERE THIS A radio program, you would be hearing the opening bars of Darius Milhaud's 1923 African-chic spectacle *La créa-tion du monde*, The Creation of the World. When it was first performed as a ballet in Paris, with a scenario by the Simultaneist poet Blaise Cendrars and sets and costumes by the Cubist inno-vator Fernand Léger, the high-point of the Parisian infatuation with jazz, or *Le Jazz* as it was referred to at the time, had al-ready passed. It had been only one fashionable fad among others briefly toyed with before being cast aside in the restless quest for new idioms and modes of artistic expression by the cultural avant-garde of the time. Others had cocked an ear to jazz before Milhaud, such as Stravinsky in his musical impressions of Rag-time, or Poulenc with his *Rapsodie nègre*, full of pseudo-African mumbo-jumbo, in much the same way that later on Ravel would concoct a hodge-podge of mock-Chinese and French in his *L'en-fant et les sortileges*. They were all playful forays into exotic ter-rain, all equally noncommittal when it came to the authenticity of the cultural sources, African American or otherwise. The atti-tude was one of an omnivorous appetite of tasting and sampling, of what is sometimes referred to as cultural slumming, typical of a mode of cultural consumption equally prevalent in 1920s Paris as in New York in the days of the Harlem Renaissance.

When Milhaud wrote his Creation of the World he had done his share of slumming in both places. In addition to the adulter-ated sounds of what Paris knew as "Le Jazz," Milhaud had been to Harlem joints and listened to blues singers like Bessie Smith and stride pianists like Willie "The Lion" Smith and James P. Johnson. More than any of his French fellow composers he had gone out to seek the genuine article and become the most alert practitioner of "Le Jazz" in his own writing of music. Yet a par-adox remains. Much as he had exposed himself to genuine early forms of jazz, when upon his return to Paris he regurgitated what he had so eagerly taken in, the sounds of jazz were not meant to evoke the nervous modernity of New York, the skyscraper mys-tique that informed so many European visions of an imagined America in the 1920s. Instead, as the soundscape to his evoca-tion of a world at the stage of its creation, the music called forth an image of a mythical primordial Africa in much the same way as African masks, which had been all the rage in Paris in the early twentieth century, and had inspired the visual language of painters such as Picasso. What Milhaud did was recontextualize a music that many would identify with the modernity of Amer-ica, and reconceive it as a music representing an imagined Africa mediated through America's black population, a remembered Africa as it kept inspiring its far-away descendants.

This is even more remarkable if we remember that at the same time American composers in their quest for a truly American musical idiom recognized jazz as precisely the material they were looking for. Composers like George Gershwin or the lesser known black composer William Still wrote music that in its to-nality, sonority, and syncopation resembles Milhaud, yet in their case served a radically different musical program. The program ironically had been outlined for them in the late nineteenth cen-tury by a visiting European composer, Antonin Dvořák, a leader in the international movement that sought to infuse the writing of music with a national voice, rooted in local traditions. While in the United States, Dvořák in his teaching and writing had reminded Americans that the music of America's black population might provide them with the folk traditions that he, and others like him, had found in ethnomusical traditions in their own national settings. It was an amazingly radical suggestion at the time, when America's black population was far from being seen as a natural component of America's social texture. In 1893, for instance, Dvořák advocated his views in the *New York Times*, when its pages were regularly filled with news of Negroes being lynched all over the American South.[1] It may have seemed an odd suggestion at the time, strangely out of place and time. Yet it was not long before American composers would take him up on his advice.

Gershwin made his first serious foray into black music in 1922, with the vaudeville opera *Blue Monday Blues*. Set on 135th Street in Harlem, this brief one-acter tells of a woman who shoots the man who's done her wrong, or so she thinks. The arias lack the verve of the best Gershwin tunes, awkwardly shuffling among the conventions of European operetta, Yiddish musical theater, and black musicals like Will Marion Cook's *In Dahomey*, a work, incidentally, inspired by Dvořák's *New World* symphony.[2] In addition to its cultural hybridity, Gershwin's *Blue Monday Blues* had a whiff of minstrelsy about it: white singers performed in black-face, and Paul Whiteman's smooth-timbred orchestra provided something other than an authentic Harlem sound. But Gershwin was learning as he went along. Commissioned by Paul Whiteman, who saw it as his mission to give jazz a quasi-classical respectability, and aided by Ferde Grofé in orchestrating the piece, Gershwin wrote *Rhapsody in Blue*, premiered in 1924 to general critical acclaim. Having come into his own as an acknowledged American composer he would go on to write his 1925 piano concerto and his 1928 *An American in Paris*. Jazz, in these compositions, was one of the ingredients along with the additional sounds of modernity, first explored by Edgar Varèse and George Antheil, in a music that was widely seen and welcomed as representative of America. Here we had a musical vision of contemporary America, a "musical America," as the eponymous journal that had carried that name as almost its program since its founding in 1898, had advocated. Echoing Dvořák's call, the journal epitomized the quest for musical nationalism, or rather for a rooted cosmopolitanism in music, on a par with the best in contemporary music written in Europe. If Gershwin had carried the ambition to achieve this aim in the area of symphonic music, he would go on to fulfill the dream of writing the "great American opera" when, in the mid-1930s, he finished writing *Porgy and Bess*. It was the fulfillment of a dream in more ways than one. Not only had it been Gershwin's dream to write an opera that could vie with the best in the established European canon while at the same time imbuing it with Americanness, he had at the same time fulfilled a more general American dream of cultural transnationalism, a dream that had inspired a generation of cultural nationalists around the time of World War I. Most famously in the pages of the influential, but short-lived, journal *The Seven Arts*, intellectuals such as Randolph Bourne, Van Wyck Brooks, or Waldo Frank had called for an American cultural emancipation, for a coming-of-age in which the United States should wrest itself free from Europe's, particularly England's, cultural tutelage, and find its own national voice. Their call contained a strange paradox. If the aim was for America's creative talent to explore and find an American cultural identity, the way to that end was a transcendence of the multiplicity of transplanted Europes represented by its variegated immigrant populations. They saw it as their mission to transcend the many ethnic voices and identities and to reach a stage of transnationalism, weaving the many discordant immigrant voices and identities into one transcendent American voice. America's national identity would be unlike Europe's mosaic of national identities, aiming for a new synthesis that merged the national and the transnational into one.

Gershwin, in writing *Porgy and Bess*, had powerfully contributed to achieving this aim. The idea of writing a full-scale

opera had preoccupied Gershwin for years. The arts patron
Otto Kahn—chairman of the board of the Metropolitan Opera,
prime mover of Jazz Age culture, old friend of Richard Strauss—
spurred him on, inviting him to write a "jazz grand opera" for
the Met. Gershwin concluded, however, that the Met's staff singers could never master the idiom; a true jazz opera could be sung
only by a black cast. That was a radical, if not crucial, position to
take, if the issue was to create a transnational culture. He broke
through established racial compartments, opening up a stage for
black artists on an equal footing with whites. More generally,
he accomplished a feat in reaching toward what we might call a
postethnic culture, a feat in cross-ethnic empathy. Here we had
a work composed by a second-generation Jewish immigrant, im-
mersing himself in a world first evoked in *Porgy*, a novel by a
white Southerner, Dubose Heyward, but enriched by Gershwin's
eager exploration of the life and culture of blacks living on the
Georgia sea islands. Exploring cultural exoticism and alterity,
he managed at the same time to make the cultural difference his
own, appropriating a cultural language for purposes of his own
artistic expression.

The word "postethnic," as I use it here, may seem like an
anachronism, a word moved backward in time from the 1990s.[3]
Then it first appeared in the nationwide debate about multiculturalism, a debate not unlike the way multiculturalism was revisited in a number of European countries. On both sides of the
Atlantic multiculturalism as a program for coping with ethnic
diversity was seen as counterproductive, as unduly compartmen-
talizing ethnic groups, locking them within their own cultural
particularisms. Trends that since the 1960s had been welcomed
as strides toward cultural emancipation, encouraging ethnic
groups to take pride in their diverse cultural identities, were now
seen as leading to cultural fragmentation and splintering. As
American historian Arthur Schlesinger saw the result, it was one
of disuniting America.[4] A powerful counterargument—for example, by cultural historian David Hollinger—pleaded in behalf of

promoting postethnicity, as a program and a policy to educate Americans in cultural empathy across ethnic lines. If universities wished to engage in identity politics, they should offer a version where black studies, women's studies, Native American Studies, and the like should no longer be in-group enclaves, but instead offer introductions into the many lives as they were led across ethnic divides. If this approach held out an ideal, it was one that we may rightfully recognize in George Gershwin's daring exercise in cross-ethnic empathy.

That was not, however, how his opera was initially received. Gershwin was seen as having crossed too many lines without a proper passport. Leftwing critics attacked what they saw as white exploitation of black material. Gershwin's racial ambiguities, his miscegenating mixture of Western-European, African American, and Russian-Jewish materials, were seen as problematic. Duke Ellington for one made the point that *Porgy and Bess* was not a true and authentic Negro Opera. As for Gershwin's blurring of genre lines, composer Virgil Thomson concluded: "I don't mind his being a light composer and I don't mind his trying to be a serious one. But I do mind his falling between two stools."[5] Falling between two stools was, in fact, the essence of Gershwin's genius. He led at all times a double life: as music-theater professional and concert composer, as highbrow artist and lowbrow entertainer, as all-American kid and immigrants' son, as white man and "white Negro."

As it was, though, nothing in the end could stop Gershwin's folk opera from becoming an American classic. Many of its songs turned into evergreens and became part of the great American songbook, the canon of its great entertainment tunes, rendered and transformed time and again by popular singers and musicians, black and white alike. At the same time in its afterlife it conquered the great opera stages of the world, from New York's Metropolitan Opera to the Scala, from the Glyndebourne Festival to opera stages in Vienna, Leningrad, and Moscow. Interesting things happened on the way, testifying to the cultural freedom that the opera opened up to its performers, making room for them to bring their creative agency to bear. British conductor Simon Rattle, for example, in the Glyndebourne production, had stopped the rehearsals asking the cast to teach him the intricacies of their style, their sense of beat and rhythm. He asked them, in other words, to teach him how to breathe life into the work as only they knew how.[6]

The opera was further helped along in gaining a worldwide audience through the panoply of technical means of cultural transmission, through gramophone recordings and radio, through film and television productions. American cultural diplomacy had its own role to play, particularly in the context of the Cold War. If the point was to disseminate an image of the United States in its cultural richness and variety, *Porgy and Bess* along with American Jazz, American painting and ballet, American writing and photography, showed the United States as creatively engaged in mastering the many problems of a society in the throes of modernization.

Gershwin's opera of course was only one musical representation of America, complex, mercurial, and multilayered. It could be unpacked and repackaged as the occasion demanded. It did provide its publics with a view of a musical America, but it was not alone in doing this. We mentioned jazz, we mentioned the repertoire of great American songs produced by what is succinctly known as Tin Pan Alley, the popular music industry. Younger generations growing up in war-ravaged European countries eagerly took in American popular music as so many sounds of modernity and vitality, providing them with models for constructing their own private worlds and identities shared with their peers. In their eyes the United States became that imaginary realm that they could hear and picture for themselves through their simple exposure to American cultural fads and fashions, carried by Hollywood films, American advertising, consumer products, radio programs, and gramophone records. Without political agency, outside the conduit of a conscious American cultural diplomacy, all these sights and sounds had washed across Europe as so many signs of an American cultural sway that slowly but irresistibly established itself in the wake of America's rise to world power.

One specific constellation of sight and sound will occupy us from here on, a composite that my title more specifically refers to: Musical America, the imagined America that is carried by one of America's cultural products in particular—its musicals. If there is a Hollywood America conveyed by film, there is equally an America, or should I say there are Americas, represented by Broadway musicals. Of course, in the late nineteenth and early twentieth centuries Americans had never been without musical entertainment, but rather than presenting them with a musical America, they had been offered musical Englands by way of the highly popular Victorian fare of Gilbert and Sullivan productions, or belle epoque musical Europes in Viennese operetta. Despite its roots in European popular stage productions such as operetta, as a typically American genre the musical came into its own in the 1920s. In the grand American manner it creatively merged European inspirations with local traditions, such as vaudeville and the American revue with its rich repertoire of songs popularized via the market for sheet music first and radio later on. The revue had known its most vibrant efflorescence in the 1920s in Florenz Ziegfeld's "Follies," which lasted from 1907 to 1931, originally modeled on the *Folies Bergère* in Paris. The signature of the Follies had been the chorus line, eye-catching and erotically clothed women whose synchronized dancing echoed the exciting Paris precursor of the Can-Can, but would go on to receive its American transformation in the cinematic choreography of Busby Berkeley in the 1930s. There were African American revues as well. Among the most notable was *Shuffle Along*, with music and lyrics by Noble Sissle and Eubie Blake, which debuted in 1921 on Broadway and ran for 484 performances. The cast of the show included Paul Robeson, with a young Josephine Baker in the chorus. Because of its success,

Shuffle Along helped inspire a fad in the 1920s for revues starring black singers and dancers. It was a fad that early on crossed
the ocean and would find eager audiences in Paris. The deepest
impact of the revues, however, was on early musical comedy, a
homegrown alternative to European-style operettas. The entertainer most responsible for the birth of musicals drenched in
Americana was George M. Cohan, an Irish-Catholic American in
spite of what his name seemed to suggest, and in spite of the fact
that it was Jewish song-writers, lyricists, and entertainers who
perfected the modern musicals of the 1920s and beyond. Cohan,
the composer of songs like "The Yankee Doodle Boy," "You're a
Grand Old Flag," "Give My Regards to Broadway," and "Over
There," linked vaudeville with ragtime. And he used urban slang
and contemporary settings to create stories and characters that
could not exist anywhere except New York.

Merging these disparate sources into one, the American musical burst onto the stage with a bang: Jerome Kern's and Oscar
Hammerstein's 1927 *Show Boat*. The musical, based on Edna
Ferber's best-selling novel from 1926, was the first "book" musical in which the characters and the story were closely linked
to the songs. *Show Boat* adopted the style of Europe's operettas
to explore the legends and darker undercurrents of America's
past. More specifically, it dealt with the themes of racism and
race miscegenation, not the usual topics for Broadway musicals
or popular entertainment more generally. Songs like "Ol' Man
River" and "Can't Help Lovin' That Man," with their reliance
on the blues and on African American vernacular, foreshadowed
Gershwin's *Porgy and Bess*. *Show Boat* became one of the few
musicals from the 1920s and '30s to be continually revived after
World War II, in the United States and abroad. It was twice made
into a film, in 1936 by Universal Pictures in black-and white,
and in 1951 by MGM, in sumptuous color but highly sanitized
when it came to the black-and-white of race relations. The 1936
version of *Show Boat* is considered by many film critics to be one
of the classic film musicals of all time, and one of the best stage-

to-film adaptations ever made. Frank S. Nugent of the *New York Times* called it "one of the finest musical films we have seen."[7]

If this is an example of the happy symbiosis between the stage, the silver screen, and later television and DVD, it also testifies to the American mastery of the tools of mass dissemination of its cultural products. It helps account for the global conquest of markets for the American musical. Yet it is not simply a matter of additional media being brought to the task of disseminating one original product. There is, as Nugent reminds us, the matter of adaptation, of creative translation from one medium into another. There is a creative challenge there that was taken up early on in the United States, bringing to life a parallel universe for musicals to flourish in. In addition to the Broadway musical a new genre came to life, that of the Hollywood musical. It would have its golden age in the years of the Great Depression, with its mixture of realism and cynical comment, as in famous songs like "We're In the Money" and "Remember My Forgotten Man," with its stark sets inspired by German expressionism. There is also "Brother, Can You Spare a Dime" from the 1931 musical *New Americana*, by lyricist E. Y. "Yip" Harburg and composer Jay Gorney. If there was a "musical America" represented here, it was one mixing the temporary oblivion held out by Hollywood's dream factory and a daring engagement with the social anxieties of the time. Busby Berkeley was the creative mind able to straddle the divide. For the *Gold Diggers of 1933* film he choreographed with equal mastery the dreams of money and affluence in the song "We're In the Money" and the downbeat "Remember My Forgotten Man," where he brought to bear his memories of the 1932 War Veterans "Bonus" March in Washington. In order for Berkeley to realize his choreographic visions the cinematic genre of the backstage musical was developed, basically two films rolled into one, with a narrative part set aside for the plot, and choreographed sections for Berkeley's dance sequences to unfold. Given this creative space, Berkeley developed a cinematic language that presented chorus line dancers as only a camera could see them, producing abstract configurations of stunning kaleidoscopic power.

Until the late 1930s, Depression-era gloom left its mark on popular culture. The stage production and film version of *The Wizard of Oz* played on the conspiratorial views that had inspired populism as a political movement and sentiment, with "Wicked Witches of the East" and "West," respectively, representing the powers of the world of finance concentrated in Wall Street, and of exploitative extraction industries as these had ravaged the West. In the film version a girl named Dorothy, played by a young and radiant Judy Garland, is transported from her drab, gray Kansas farm to the enchanted Technicolor land of Oz. The wizard turns out to be a charlatan, in the great American tradition of the Confidence Man. Still, he has an important lesson to teach. People, he says, don't need a wizard to give them a heart, a brain, or courage. All they need to do is look inside themselves. Inner strength, not a social miracle, is the wizard's (and Hollywood's) key to salvation. So a movie that begins with Dorothy imagining a fantasy world somewhere over the rainbow (in Yip Harburg's memorable lines) ends with her back in Kansas, proclaiming that "there's no place like home." It set the tone for a celebration of the common folk and the "Common Man," as it had more generally inspired the artistic production of the time. Most memorably so in Aaron Copland's work in what he himself would later refer to as his vernacular period, in *Rodeo, Appalachian Spring, Fanfare for the Common Man,* and his *Lincoln Portrait.* That tone of celebration, if not cheery optimism, was most evident in another revisit of the American heartland, in Rodgers and Hammerstein's 1943 production of *Oklahoma!* With the end of the Depression and a regained sense of national purpose and mission in World War II, America had taken heart and found courage within itself, projecting it onto the folk in its heartland. It was a smash hit and ran for five years and a record-shattering 2,212 performances. Its popularity was enhanced by the cast album, which sold more than a million copies when originally released. Albums henceforth would remain instrumental in establishing Broadway musicals as an essential component of America's wartime and postwar culture, helping it to conquer foreign publics along the way.

What made *Oklahoma!* special was its sophisticated fusion of music, dance, and drama. Still, for all its stylistic modernity, *Oklahoma!* was an exercise in Americana. It was a celebration of the end of the Depression. In 1939 John Steinbeck had portrayed an Oklahoma in *The Grapes of Wrath* that, like the rest of America, was still marked by scarcity and deprivation. Now, in 1943, Rodgers and Hammerstein created a mythical Oklahoma that, unlike Steinbeck's dustbowl, was a bountiful land where the corn grew as high as an elephant's eye. Audiences elsewhere could also appreciate the music and the tale. When *Oklahoma!* opened in London in 1947, it was as popular as it had been in the United States. By the 1950s the show was drawing large crowds in France and Italy and would soon be performed throughout the world. When I first met my wife in the late 1960s, I was welcomed to her house by a parrot intoning "Oh, what a beautiful morning." *Oklahoma!* was thus a global as well as an American success story, with publics both human and avian. At the same time it powerfully projected a musical America for all the world to behold. And as the American musical conquered the world, an older story of the cultural reception of American forms of entertainment by others repeated itself. Not only did they function at the same level of "mere" entertainment, making for a pleasant evening out, they moved up the scale of cultural and critical appreciation. Thus the successful Broadway musical *Guys and Dolls*, based on Damon Runyon's ribald sketches of Manhattan street life, moved to London to open, in 1982, not as a commercial West End production—as one might have expected—but on the stage of the National Theatre, the pinnacle of British drama. It was a cultural "first." The musical was directed by Richard Eyre, one of the all-time great directors of the National Theatre, who once admitted to having greater affinity with American popular culture, having grown up with it, than with the hallowed canon of British theater.[8]

At the same time, we should remember, American musicals daringly ventured into appropriating foreign materials, constructing fantasy versions of Paris in *An American in Paris*, of a late Weimar Berlin in *Cabaret*, an exoticized Thailand in *The King and I*, a Victorian England and its class distinctions in *My Fair Lady*, an Austria on the eve of Nazi takeover in *The Sound of Music*, or the South Pacific in a musical by that name influenced by Puccini's *Madame Butterfly*. Increasingly for the American musical the world was its oyster. Any country's past would do, any literary repertoire could serve the purpose. Ovid's story of Pyramus and Thisbe, rendered twice by Shakespeare, once as farce in his *Midsummer Night's Dream,* and once as dramatic romance in *Romeo and Juliet*, underwent its American appropriation in Leonard Bernstein's *West Side Story*. In this mercurial expansiveness not every American musical therefore carried a musical America. Yet, undeniably, there always was an American touch, an American way with artistic creation, that left an American imprint on the narratives it told, whether on the stage, in film, or in music. Exposing foreign publics to the generic Americanness of its cultural production, it set cultural standards and created cultural formats for others to emulate. If for generations among America's creative elites Europe had been the imposing father figure that needed to be killed for the American progeny to come into its own, the tables had now been turned.

One way to go was for foreign countries to be as good as the Americans, as expert in finding mass audiences, yet replace the Americanness with foreign content. And many foreign productions show that it is possible successfully to take up the challenge. The ultimate sign of success is then for foreign productions to cross the Atlantic and to "make it" on Broadway. As it is, there have been successful imports from England, from the late 1950s–early 1960s on, purveying Britishness as in Lionel Bart's *Oliver!*

or in Julian Slade's and Dorothy Reynold's *Salad Days*, or from France, using French content as in the case of Claude-Michel Schoenberg's *Les Misérables* or *Miss Saigon*. Soon, it turned out, musical productions could travel on their own and no longer needed the appeal of their national origin. A good case in point is Andrew Lloyd Webber's *Jesus Christ Superstar*, produced on Broadway and available on record before it was staged in London. This also goes to illustrate the further point that increasingly the production of musicals has become an international business. It was after all an Englishman, Cameron Mackintosh, who internationally produced Schoenberg's French musicals. Today's production of musicals aims for markets, where London's West End or New York's Broadway are mere nodal points in a larger picture. At the same time, though, Broadway has kept its full symbolic weight as being the ultimate yardstick for success. It still sets standards for others to follow.

Ultimately, then, if imitation is the tribute one has to pay to success, isn't there one further step in this process, beyond imitation? Can we imagine a foreign emancipation from the American model, a hybrid form consisting in an appropriation of the many Americas that publics have been exposed to while consuming America's mass culture but mixed in with critical refractions as forms of cultural resistance? In order to illustrate this point I suggest a widening of what so far I have understood by the term "musical America." In our present day and age, with the rise of the World Wide Web and YouTube, there is a constant barrage of musical Americas in the form of music videos. For the sake of my argument we may conceive of them as condensed musicals, telling short stories, mixing visual imagery with music. In that format, more easily than in the expensive stage production of musicals, we come across examples that rely on globalized forms of visual entertainment, often of a markedly American imprint, while rearranging the material to produce statements of cultural resistance, if not cultural anti-Americanism, in the face of a threatening Americanization.

I have two illustrations of the complex interactions between the European appropriation of American cultural forms, and their rearrangement in defense of the variety of Europe's local cultural identities. Both are visual documents, music videos produced in Europe, one in the Basque country in Spain, the other in Romania in the wake of the toppling of its communist regime. The Basque video, which I discussed in the previous chapter, in itself represents an act of cultural emancipation from the cultural hegemony imposed under the Franco dictatorship. The lyrics are in Basque, and the station broadcasting the video has all-Basque programming. This may suggest localism, if not cultural provincialism. Nothing would be further from the truth. What we have here is a perfect example of "glocalisation," to use Roland Robertson's neologism.[9] The claim made in this video is on behalf of the authenticity of regional cultures struggling to survive in a world threatened by the homogenizing forces of globalization. Yet the medium of communication, the music video and the musical genre, testifies to the impact of precisely those forces as much as it protests against them. There is much irony in all this, but most important is the fact that what is shown as modernity truly revives a long repertoire of European cultural anti-Americanism. America *is* modernity, and the long history of European resistance to America is truly a story of resisting the onslaught of modernity on Europe's checkered map of regional and/or national cultures.[10]

The Romanian music video, a coproduction by Puya and Rap singer Connect-R, is called "My Americandrim" (My American Dream). It takes the viewer back to the heady days of the toppling of the Ceausescu regime, eagerly reported on American TV news. Connect-R, who in other work shows he can be the perfect local replica of an American gangster rapper, here takes a disabused view of life in Romania after the revolution, presented as a landscape of broken dreams with its democratic promise unfulfilled. The refrain—in English—keeps repeating these lines:

I can be what i want to be
Losing my identity
Cause i got a lot of life in me
Let me live my American dream

The key words here are "losing my identity." Images and lyrics go together in showing a cultural wasteland, cut adrift, without local moorings or a sense of cultural continuity with the past, yet open to influences and cultural imports from all sides. The images build up to an indictment, not unlike the Basque video, of the pernicious impact of globalization. Yet, ironically, the message is being delivered by a man who does live his American dream in the borrowed identity of an American gangster rapper.[11]

These are only two examples of cultural reception being critically turned against its originator, of music videos as an American genre providing the language for a critique of Americanization. They come closer to doing this than any form of musical America on stage that comes to my mind. Unless we go back in time to the heady days of Weimar Germany's infatuation with things American, at the height of its "Amerikanismus Debatte," and remind ourselves of Kurt Weill's and Bertold Brecht's *Rise and Fall of the City of Mahagonny*. From even before the heyday of the American musical, Brecht and Weill give us a musical America as a satire of the American Way.

[5]

A SPAGHETTI SOUTHERN: LANDSCAPES
OF FEAR IN QUENTIN TARANTINO'S
DJANGO UNCHAINED

YEARS AGO, IN *The Return of the Vanishing American,* Leslie
Fiedler explored what he saw as the reemergence of the American Indian as a central character in literary writing.[1] His title
may have referred back to the wistful construction of Native
Americans as a vanishing race, most poignantly in Edward S.
Curtis's photograph, captioned "The vanishing race," a photograph of a small group of Indians riding off into the dark, as
if in a film's closing shot. But, as Fiedler reminded his readers,
the news of the Indians' demise had been greatly exaggerated.
They had returned to a number of fields of artistic imagination,
in literature, in film, and more often than ever before as agents
of their own representation. Never mind that their return could
come in many guises; Fiedler recognized American Indian agency
in the shape of the modern hipster, blurring the features of the
returnee. Fiedler went on to suggest the space for their return as
constituting one field for American mythology to play itself out
alongside three others. He saw four main regional varieties in the
American literary imagination. Next to the Western—crucially
to do with the encounter between American Indians and white
settlers—he distinguished the Southern, the Northern, and the
Eastern. Obvious examples come to mind, such as Faulkner's im-

aginary South, or New England as imagined by Nathaniel Haw-
thorne. If they are separate genres, with their characteristic narrative tropes and typical heroes, we should guard against setting
the categories too neatly apart. Fiedler himself blurred the lines
of separation, recognizing the Red Man's features in the hipster
who, one might argue, represented the new central character in
the Eastern, the big-city novel. If Fiedler thus blurred the lines
between the Western and the Eastern, Norman Mailer had gone
there before in his creation of the White Negro, the hipster as a
black inspiration, thus merging the Eastern and the Southern, and
even the Western, into one inspirational hybrid. "A phenomenon
has appeared: the American existentialist—the hipster, (. . .)
a frontiersman in the Wild West of American night life."[2]

Now where does that leave us? In a conceptual area, for sure,
where regional mythologies meet, and mythical repertoires from
the West, the East, and the South engage in mutual permutations.
Not only was the hipster a frontiersman, he was also a Negro,
as Mailer goes on to argue: "And in this wedding of the white
and the black it was the Negro who brought the cultural dowry.
Any Negro who wishes to live must live with danger from his
first day, and no experience can ever be casual to him, no Negro
can saunter down a street with any real certainty that violence
will not visit him on his walk." Living with danger from one's
first day had been the defining feature of the American Negro's
life in the South, a life that forms the submerged narrative of the
Southern, always there, always suppressed, the dialectical opposite of the cavalier, or chivalresque, version of "civilized life" in
the South. We shall have the occasion later on to revisit this dark,
submerged narrative repertoire. But first let us take up Fiedler's
suggestive hunch and consider how his four regional genres,
in their entangled permutations, may have affected the face of
America as it was projected domestically and abroad.

Blurring and blending the genres as Americans themselves
may have done, they had at the same time a continuous interest in and awareness of boundaries setting the cultural regions

apart. They could even, playfully, make it a narrative theme and introduce an outsider's perspective into the story. A classic example is Faulkner's *Absalom, Absalom!* At one point the author has a Northerner, in fact a Canadian, ask his Harvard roommate, who is from the South: "Tell about the South. What's it like there. What do they do there. Why do they live there. Why do they live at all."[3] Similarly, in John Ford's *The Man Who Shot Liberty Valance*, a newspaper man, having pieced together the true story behind the commonly accepted version of who killed Valance, burns his notes adding this piece of wisdom: "This is the West, sir. When the legend becomes fact, print the legend."

This is a lesson that Europeans may have taken to heart in their exposure to the American imaginary. Less astute in their knowledge and awareness of America's regional diversity, they may have played fast and loose with America's cultural characteristics. Caring not for facts, but for legends, they felt free to do their own blending and blurring, projecting onto the larger canvas of America what was of specific concern to them at any given moment. Thus, ahead of Norman Mailer, Jean-Paul Sartre could recognize his existentialist hero, a man of unreflective action, in the taciturn protagonists of the Hollywood Western.[4] Similarly, he and other eager explorers of American culture, such as Boris Vian, saw a powerful example in the American urban vision of the hard-boiled novel—a subgenre of the Eastern, if you wish. The work was introduced in translation in a book series, founded by Marcel Duhamel in 1945 and published by Gallimard. The authors, most of them American, included Raymond Chandler, Dashiell Hammett, Horace McCoy, William R. Burnett, Ed McBain, Chester Himes, Lou Cameron, Jim Thompson, Rene Brabazon Raymond (under his pseudonym James Hadley Chase), and Peter Cheney. It was known as the *série noire* after the black cover of the volumes. The word *noir* then traveled and came to describe the postwar Hollywood genre of crime films. The term *film noir* is commonly believed to have been first suggested, in 1946, by the French critic Nino Frank in the journal

L'écran français.[5] The word is now common coinage among film historians on both sides of the Atlantic. The newly acquired taste in France for hard-boiled crime writing spawned a series of films, produced in the 1950s and early '60s, based on Peter Cheney's character of Lemmy Caution. Although now largely forgotten, the films were widely popular in a number of European countries and established the fame of lead-actor Eddie Constantine. Born in the United States and living in France, his American accent and laid-back acting style gave the films an ironic touch of Americanness that chimed well with the receptivity to things American in Europe at the time. They were action films basically, ending in long, almost festive brawls that left their locale a total ruin. Such cinematic magnetism as Constantine possessed fully came into its own later when Jean-Luc Godard, one of France's New Wave directors, used the Lemmy Caution character in his *Alphaville* (1965), a neo-noir science fiction film.[6] With trench coat and cigarette, Constantine more than ever before recalled the Hollywood noir character played by Humphrey Bogart.

This is just one example of how Europeans, while adopting America's repertoire of regional-cum-cultural diversity, may have felt free to rearrange what had come to them according to their own rules of canon formation. They had done so before, in the interwar years, with American jazz music—for example, in France and Germany, developing critical standards and a critical discourse for ordering the field in high and low, in genres and styles, in good and bad. They would do so again, in the 1950s, with Hollywood films, recognizing first the hands of master film makers where no one had noticed them before, then taking their cue from Hollywood in what would be the New Wave, the *Nouvelle Vague*, in 1960s French film production. Never hampered by what came naturally to Americans—a sense of cultural mooring in one variety of regional culture or another, a sense of Us and Them within the national cultural landscape—Europeans could take it all in as interchangeable faces of one larger, imaginary "America." This may have had particular force in the case of the Western, a category that Europeans had long adopted to refer especially to films set in the West; yet it never kept them from seeing in the iconic faces of the West the all-American features that they carried in their heads. Recycled for commercial pur poses, this rugged male face of the Westerner came to constitute the Marlboro Man, put in the service of a brand of cigarettes, but, more important, feeding the imagination, of Americans first, of people elsewhere later. As research has shown, to Americans the Marlboro Man represented the American West, to people elsewhere he came to be a generalized all-American icon.[7] As imagined by non-Americans, therefore, the American West may offer greater leeway to fantasies, more room for imaginative play, than would come naturally to Americans. In their playful reshuf-fling of the deck, Europeans basically play a game that Ameri-cans have played before them. It was for Americans to blend and blur the lines of genre distinction first, for Europeans to follow in their footsteps. But they have done so with a vengeance.

The Eddie Constantine French pub brawl films—we might call them *Café Noir Easterns*—are now mostly forgotten. At about the same time Italian film makers would also take a leaf from America's cultural catalog and begin producing Westerns, giving their own twist to the genre. Frowned on initially and seen as less than B-movies by film critics in both Europe and the United States, many of the films are now considered classics and have moved up the charts of critical esteem. Collectively these Ital-ian Westerns became known, disparagingly at first, appreciatively now, as spaghetti Western. They had their own authentic American hero, Clint Eastwood. Known from his supporting-cast role in the TV series *Rawhide*, in 1963 he grasped the opportunity to escape from his TV image. He signed on for the lead role in *A Fistful of Dollars*, a film to be shot in a remote region of Spain by the then rel-atively unknown Sergio Leone. The rest, to coin a phrase, is history.

The new genre soon had its own canon, based on its cinematic style, its musical scores, but most of all on its greater moral com-plexity, the unabashed violence of its stories, and the ambiguity of its heroes. Often there was tacit critique of economic power and the corruptibility of man, which gave the films a faintly political left-wing feel. In its rapid rise to international success, the spaghetti Western inspired many to join its bandwagon, in hopes of joining the ranks of its uncontested masters: Sergio Leone and Sergio Corbucci. Of the two, Corbucci is the lesser known, yet as the maker of films such as *The Great Silence* and *Django* he is of lasting influence and inspiration to younger film makers. Of the two, Corbucci is also arguably the one who most radically overturned the Western genre's conventions, witness the ending he gave to *The Great Silence*. In a scene of unprecedented violence and cruelty, a bleak ending lacking any of the heroic features of so many Westerns' climactic confrontations, the sympathetic characters are gunned down by their opponents, a bunch of greedy bounty hunters.

Leone's career most clearly tells the story of the rise from marginal beginnings in the face of derision and snobbish rejection to ultimate recognition and the acknowledgement of his mastery. Working in a cinematic genre that he had taken over from America while using a film idiom recognizably his own, he took the resulting hybrid form home in his epic masterpiece *Once upon a Time in the West*, a lavish 1968 production filmed in both the American West and the south of Spain. And, as if for good measure, in 1985 he added *Once upon a Time in America*. It was a meditation on another aspect of popular American mythology, the role of greed and violence and their uneasy coexistence with the meaning of ethnicity and friendship. It told the saga of the many immigrants who, as a literal cast of thousands, allowed Leone, in a grand gesture of farewell, to add to his oeuvre a magisterial Eastern, a spaghetti Eastern if you will.

Quentin Tarantino's Django Unchained

Tarantino's latest film, *Django Unchained*, ends in scenes of horrific violence. The ending comes in two parts, in almost two different modes. In what seems a direct reference to Corbucci's *The Great Silence*, in its desolate bleakness, Tarantino shows his hero hanging head down, about to be tortured, even castrated. It is a dramatic reversal of the plot. Having successfully penetrated into the very heart of darkness—Candieland, a Mississippi plantation run by its ruthless and sadistic owner, Calvin Candie—Django, a free black man, and Dr. King Schulz, German immigrant, master trickster and bounty hunter, are close to accomplishing their self-assigned mission of freeing Broomhilda, the love of Django's life, from slavery.[8] The mission itself, told with light and hilarious touches mixed in with ominous, blood-chilling flashes of slavery, is close to success, when the visitors' true intent is found out. Dr. Schulz, rather than giving Candieland's cruel master the sweet smell of victory, shoots him at point blank range, killing him. The two, Dr. Schulz and Django, stand no chance of escape. Dr. Schulz is killed on the spot, while Django, valiantly trying to shoot his way out of the mansion, finally finds himself outgunned and surrenders. Next we see him hanging down, in an image reminiscent of so many lynching scenes, spelling what can only be the hero's—that is, the story's—end.

But Tarantino isn't quite done yet. With true trickster's ingenuity —a tribute to his German companion and teacher's mastery— Django frees himself and, with a load of dynamite, sets off to Candieland for the final reckoning. This is part two of Tarantino's ending, where he again takes up his favorite theme of the fantasy of revenge, as memorably done before in *Inglourious Basterds*. This time Tarantino reverses the Corbucci ending and shows Django slowly taking out the inhabitants of Candieland, one by one, clearly savoring the moment. He overlooks the scene of slaughter from a mezzanine, like the avenger who suddenly materializes from the hills in so many Western movies. He saves ultimate revenge until the last: with two shots he incapacitates Stephen, the slaveholder's trusted house slave and confidant, whose coldly observant eye had seen through Dr. Schulz's ploy before he informed his master. He is the ultimate Uncle Tom turned traitor to his race. Left on the floor, he raves in impotent rage, while a burning fuse works its way toward the dynamite. Emerging from a sea of flames Django joins his Broomhilda like the victorious mythical German hero Tristan that Dr. Schulz had told him about. Once again narrative repertoires and genres merge relentlessly into one another. For good measure the reunited lovers ride off into the future to a musical score taken straight from yet another spaghetti Western, *They Call Me Trinity*.[9] Its lyrics ring in the audience's ears when it gets ready to leave the theater: "He's the guy who's the talk of the town, He's the top of the West, Always cool, he's the best." Thus, the film is replete with markers of the Western genre, including its spaghetti Western variety. But never one to be pinned down easily in clearly denoted boxes, Tarantino joyfully confounds genres, when, for example, he has Dr. Schulz praising Django's prowess as a gunman, telling him that he will be known as "the fastest gun in the South."

Thus, with such tongue-in-cheek, intertextual jokes strewn casually before the audience, is it more than fun that Tarantino is after? Is he more than the master joker out to surpass earlier Westerns in the comic mode? Undeniably there is much in his film to remind us of Mel Brooks's *Blazing Saddles*, as in the hilarious quasi–Ku Klux Klan posse getting ready for a raid, milling about on horseback fumbling with their white sheets, complaining they can't see from their slitted hoods. And doesn't Broomhilda von Shaft remind us of Brooks's Lili von Shtupp? Also, there is the hilarious unfinished, and unanswered question "What's a nih . . . ?" in response to the astounded exclamation, "Hey, the sheriff's a nih . . ." (an exclamation cut short by a clock chiming). Tarantino doesn't leave things up in the air. There are no clocks chiming to drown the n-word out. Tarantino's dialogues are full of the n-word, used by whites and blacks alike.

But my point is that Tarantino does more than that. For all his mixing of modes, genres, inspirations, he does break out of the cage of intertextuality and show us glimpses of an outside world in its full sinister grimness, a world that is truly the South as lived by its black population. There are those like David Denby who don't see this. "Yes, of course, there were killers in the Old West and cruel slave masters in the South . . . but Tarantino juices everything into gaudy pop fantasy. I enjoyed parts of 'Django Unchained' very much, but I'm surprised that anyone can take it as anything more than an enormous put-on."[10] I am not so sure. At one point in the film Calvin Candie, verbally enabled sadist that he is, holds forth on phrenology, a racist theory beloved by the Southern white elite, because it teaches that blacks were born to be slaves, as a genetically subordinate race. He tells this in answer to the question he himself raised before. Having grown up in the South surrounded by black people, like so many white people surrounded by far larger numbers of blacks, he wonders, "Why haven't they killed us all?" The answer as he sees it lies in race, lies in genetics. Tarantino sees things differently and uses his powers as a cinematographer to show what the true answer is to Candie's question.

In 2007, Tarantino discussed an idea for a form of spaghetti Western set in the U.S. pre–Civil War Deep South that he called "a southern," stating that he wanted "to do movies that deal with America's horrible past with slavery and stuff but do them like spaghetti Westerns, not like big issue movies. I want to do them like they're genre films, but they deal with everything that America has never dealt with because it's ashamed of it."[11] Tarantino later explained the genesis of the idea: "I was writing a book about Sergio Corbucci when I came up with a way to tell the story. . . . I was writing about how his movies have this evil Wild West, a horrible Wild West. It was surreal, it dealt a lot with fascism."[12]

Whatever the precise way this inspiration worked out, it allowed Tarantino to turn the "horrible Wild West" into the horrible South of slavery and racist suppression. He depicts racism in the South as a regime of fear that lurks everywhere, chillingly evoked on screen in scene after scene, with the mastery the audience remembers from earlier Tarantino films, where sadist joy builds up, savoring every minute of it, before an ear gets sliced off—as in *Reservoir Dogs*—or brains get blown out that have first figured out what the French call a quarter pounder—as in *Pulp Fiction*. Such scenes of almost tangible terror take us back to Norman Mailer's observation quoted before: "Any Negro who wishes to live must live with danger from his first day." Living in fear would be a more precise way to put it. It suggests settings replete with fearsome, literally dread-ful or fright-ful objects that send chills down one's spine by merely setting eyes on them. It suggests scenes of loitering white people whose cold, evil eyes, like a Gorgon's gaze petrifying everyone caught in it, monitor public space in the South. It is a monitoring gaze, though, felt only if one is a black person in the South and trained to respect the emblems and signs of the white man's displeasure. Whites may in fact be unaware most of the time of the signal structures they have set up to regulate the behavior of blacks. They literally inhabit a different world. And it is Tarantino's mastery to make his audience see those signal structures as if through the eyes of blacks. In scene after scene we feel our hair stand up in fear, being given a vicarious sense of life in the South as lived by blacks. If Tarantino has produced a Southern it is a topsy-turvy one, bringing the dark side of life in the South, and the submerged and suppressed narratives that go with it, into everyone's full view.

Landscapes of Fear

A recent study might serve as the travel guide to the American South as seen through the eyes of black people. In *The Properties of Violence: Claims to Ownership in Representations of Lynching*, Sandy Alexandre addresses this central question: "What (and where) is Arcadia to African Americans?"[13] Can they fully share, on the same footing as whites, in the Western aesthetic tradition of awe in the face of nature as an emanation of the

Sublime? Do they share with whites the American pastoral ideal? Her book argues the opposite. She quotes Evelyn White's memorable phrase: "My genetic memory of ancestors hunted down and preyed upon in rural settings counters my fervent hopes of finding peace in the wilderness. Instead of the solace and comfort I seek, I imagine myself in the country as my forebears were— exposed, vulnerable, and unprotected—a target of cruelty and hate."[14] This idea of a genetic memory, of a store of memories as warning signals shared by a group defined by its genetic—that is, racial—features defines Alexandre's intellectual quest. She traces what imprint the "polluting touch of the white man"—a phrase she takes from Angelina Weld Grimké's short story *Blackness*— has left on the Southern landscape. In Grimké's story the narrator confesses, having heard the story of a gruesome lynching, that no tree will ever be quite the same to him again. But as Alexandre makes clear throughout her book, this is how the black people's "genetic memory" got formed. She revisits a popular song ("Strange Fruit," written by the Jewish American teacher and poet Lewis Allen, and later made famous by the singer Billy Holiday) to introduce the reader to her central theme: the horrific gap between the idyllic landscape—where plants and trees bear real flowers and fruit—and the "strange and bitter crop" of swinging black bodies hanging from these same trees.[15] Alexandre then looks at lynching photographs, from the National Center for Civil and Human Rights collection, published as *Without Sanctuary*.[16] It powerfully and gruesomely expresses the extent to which lynchings have tainted the Southern pastoral, turning it into something unnatural and brutal that belies any bucolic claims. In chapter after chapter, revisiting black literary writing, she evokes this peculiar outlook, twisted and contorted by the remembered history of torment and cruelty. Whites may have been the agents of this regime, their eyes may have been the instruments of the lethal Medusa gaze, petrifying every black person it alighted on, yet these same whites have blissfully lived their lives in a parallel universe of chivalric gallantry and fine manners.

Alexandre's book convincingly traces the outlines of a genre of cultural representation that turns established views of "the Southern" upside down. It explores life in the South as experienced by its black people, thus literally opening the eyes of outsiders to "what the South is like" to its *black* inhabitants. And precisely this, I would argue, is what Quentin Tarantino's *Django Unchained* manages to achieve. In addition to its many stylistic and genre quotations, its irrepressible and joyous intertextuality, it does consistently return to perhaps its central mission: giving its audience the feel of an American South, of a regime of fear and oppression as experienced by the oppressed. His narrative ploy—a true master stroke—for achieving this is having a free black man on horseback, riding rough-shod over the many hair-trigger devices planted by the white South. Identifying with this hero, whose very appearance, whose every step is a transgression, the audience is made aware of all the lurking threats and dangers besetting him. Riding into the small Texas town of Daughtry, Django is shown riding past hair triggers that would normally spell terror and retaliation. Thus, as the camera follows him, a noose appears, from right to left across the screen, hanging ready, while dumbfounded whites can do no more than mutter: "A nigger on a horse!" Entering a bar, there is a shout: "Get that nigger outa here." Django—and Dr. Schulz—ignore it. Later scenes in this journey to the heart of darkness recall the acts that have tainted the landscape forever in the black people's imagination. Lashings of blacks tied to a tree, a cowering black man up in a tree beleaguered by hounds, and later to be thrown before them to the sadistic joy of poor whites loitering around. In these sequences showing Django transgressing, trampling underfoot the entire rulebook meant to keep blacks in their place, there are hair-raising moments: in one instance whites, exuding anger, and still unaware of the true hierarchy that confronts them, tell Django, who is about to follow his German companion and their white hosts on horseback: "Name of the game is catch-up, not keep-up, nigger." Sadistic sniggering all around, before the true relations of power dawn on them, and Django, now on horse-back and in cool control, is shown looking down on them. Seen from similar camera angles, Tarantino goes on creating a series of transgressions that would normally have brought torture and death to the transgressor. They are each chilling moments, yet always at the same time moments of revenge and victory for Django. That makes it all, up to and including the final climatic moments of the film, a fantasy, a fairy tale. Yet at the same time it also takes the audience on a tour of what made (and can still make) racism work as a system of social control. That is what ultimately makes Tarantino's film a Southern, albeit one of a rad-ically revamped nature, a Southern centering on Southern blacks, not whites. We might call this new genre flippantly Southern *noir*.

What Fantasy, What Revenge?

It is good at this point to engage in one final comparison and to remind ourselves of what real transgressions of the Southern codes for proper black behavior, in the not too distant past, have meant for the transgressor. Sandy Alexandre devotes one chap-ter of her book to the sad case of Emmett Till. He was a black boy, born and raised in Chicago. A photograph shows him as a free-spirited young man, with a winning expression of enterprise and self-confidence. He appears as the embodiment of someone who had lived the dream of the North that had led so many blacks to leave the South in two great waves of migration north-ward, cast in the light of an Old Testament exodus to a land of freedom. Although not without initial misgivings, in 1955 his mother judged the time had come for Emmett to have a taste of the white world's ways of sending their children to summer camp, to enjoy life in the "great outdoors" and get an education in pastoral enjoyment. It was not to be. Unaccustomed to the ways of the Jim Crow South, Emmett Till, who had allegedly wolf whistled to a white woman, was atrociously murdered and thrown into the Tallahatchie River. As his mother would write later, "[F]or a free-spirited boy who lived to be outdoors, there was so much possibility, so much adventure in (the wide-open spaces of) Mississippi . . . . Mississippi represented freedom."[17] It turned out the opposite way. In his comportment, Emmett Till had brought a bit of Chicago with him to Mississippi, and such interspatial/interideological mixing just would not be tolerated by the likes of Emmett's murderers, who had their own strictly schematic understanding of the mutually exclusive differences between the urban North and the rural South.[18] In her tireless efforts to have the heinous crime brought out before a general public and to expose Southern racism for what it was, particularly after the murderers had been quickly acquitted by a local all-white jury, Emmett's mother used two photographs to particularly great effect, one the "before" photograph of the dapper young man, the other taken after Emmett's dead body had been spit up by the river, bloated and mutilated almost beyond recognition. This photographic reconstruction of the tragedy reinforced a reading of the cultural contrast between the North as a safe haven for dreams of freedom versus the South as the land without sanctuary. Thus, the gruesome story of Emmett Till was rendered especially powerful because its photographic record reinforced the paradigmatic reading of the contrast of North versus South. It did so because Emmett Till was a Northerner who had stepped outside the boundaries of his sanctuary, and who, because of his ignorance of the unwritten code of black compliance enforced by the cold, Gorgon gaze of the white community, ended up as a cruelly murdered victim of the South, forever frozen in the picture of his bloated face.

This story, it may be clear, is a tale of real events mixed in with illusions and dreams, such as visions of the South as a good place for a black Northern city boy to spend the summer, or of the North as the new land of liberty. Yet the tragedy as it took place was real enough, and so was the revenge of Emmett Till's mother. Relying on gruesome photographic evidence she unrelentingly dragged the South before the court of international public opinion. Through photographic mediation she managed to bring to life, not her son, but an international community of shared grief and indignation. Surely, this was a virtual community, yet one that could manage to change the course of history and sustain a civil rights movement as it was taking shape in the United States.

Is it conceivable that such a twisted story of illusions and fantasies, having real effects, might have been on the back of Quentin Tarantino's mind when conceiving of his film *Django*? Could similar stories of American regions and regional cultures clashing have informed his fantasies, not of a Northerner, but of a Westerner trespassing on Southern cultural turf? Could, for that matter, the stories of the freedom rides from the North invading the South in the early 1960s have resonated with him? Are there echoes of *Mississippi Burning* in Django? For someone with Tarantino's intertextual mind the answer to all of the above is most likely yes. Much more strongly so than in his previous revenge fantasy *Inglourious Basterds*, there certainly is a seething anger in Django that runs parallel to the anger that inspired Mamie Till's revenge, or that sizzles through *Mississippi Burning*. More clearly than ever before in his work, Tarantino may have broken out of the pleasure garden of intertextual and cross-genre games and turned his talents to the injustices and torments of the real world. Is Tarantino getting real?

[6]

FREAKS ON DISPLAY: A TALE OF
EMPATHY AND OSTRACISM

What we call monsters are not so to God, who sees in the immensity
of his work the infinity of forms that he has comprised in it. . . . We
call contrary to nature what happens contrary to custom; nothing is
anything but according to nature, whatever it may be. Let this universal
and natural reason drive out of us the error and astonishment that
novelty brings us.
—Michel de Montaigne, "Of a Monstrous Child" ("Au sujet d'un
enfant monstrueux," *Essais*, Chapitre 30, Livre II, 1580–88)

Und wenn du lange in einen Abgrund blickst, blickt der Abgrund auch
in dich hinein [When you stare long into an abyss, the abyss stares into
you as well].
—Friedrich Nietzsche, *Jenseits von Gut und Böse*, Aphorism 146, 1886

Introduction: Freak Shows and
the Health of the Social Body

IN HIS 1962 *Freaks*, Leslie Fiedler laments the disappearance
of a form of popular entertainment that he fondly remembers
from his youth, the freak show. As he sees it, its demise may have
had to do with a secular change in the public's appetites, tastes,
and sensitivities. No longer was it seen as acceptable behavior
to laugh at other people's birth defects, or unabashedly to pa-

rade the grotesque variations on the human body before an eager public willing to pay the price of admission.[1]

The timing of Fiedler's book was not without irony. While looking back at the history of freak shows, he did not see a wave coming, if not a tidal change, that would wash across the cultural landscape of the 1960s and would redeem the appeal of freaks and everything they stood for in terms of transgression, cultural inversion, and festive rebellion. Freak as a verb (as in "freak out") and a noun came to stand for cultural options that a youthful generation eagerly explored. As a sign of the times a film was re-released that following its first release in 1932 was seen as too shocking and was rapidly withdrawn: Tod Browning's *Freaks*. Once given its second lease on life, it rapidly turned into a cult movie. In the more culturally tolerant and morally permissive atmosphere of the 1960s the film's message was finally received as intended. Using the format of Hollywood's playful genre of the backstage musical, pioneered by Busby Berkeley, *Freaks* can be seen as a backstage freak show. It shows the daily life of circus artists, freaks—or human prodigies—among them, as it unfolds behind the stage of their public performance. The narrative is a variation on the traditional Hollywood romance, given a twist by the fact that this time the one to fall in love is a dwarf, Hans, and the lady of his dreams the trapeze artist and femme fatale Cleopatra. As the melodrama unfolds it turns out that Cleopatra marries Hans for the money he has inherited. Not only does she openly ridicule and denigrate him, she also starts to poison him. That is when the circus community of freaks bands together. If one of them is done harm, all are hurt. In an act of solidarity, restoring the moral order of their community, they take cruel revenge, maiming Cleopatra in ways that forever turn her into a bird woman, a freak that will henceforth be part of the show to titillate the visitors. All is well that ends well: at the end of the film Hans and his devoted fellow-midget Frieda declare everlasting love for each other.

In seeing to it that justice is done and Cleopatra will get her just desert, the film more readily enticed 1960s publics than publics in the 1930s to empathize with the freaks, and to take their point of view. More important, the 1960s public saw through the act of cruel revenge at the end of the film and took the point that freaks can be *made*, that people can be "enfreaked" or turn themselves into freaks. This is precisely what set the tone and language of much of the cultural revolution in the 1960s, and from there could lead straight to the gradual self-enfreakment of pop stars like David Bowie or Michael Jackson.[2] Among the many mercurial transformations of his public image is a depiction of Bowie as a 1920s carnival freak in the lurid cover drawing for his 1974 album *Diamond Dogs*. Similarly, for the ongoing construction of his public persona Michael Jackson as well had taken his cues from the world of the freak sideshows, a world of which he had acquired intimate knowledge. Many freak performers had indeed reached stardom and were known across the United States by such grandiloquent names as General Tom Thumb, a famous nineteenth-century Lilliputian, or Prince Randian, in a manner of theatrical self-construction that Robert Bogdan has called the aggrandized mode of freak presentation. That Prince Randian, an armless, legless, writhing body, was also known as "the human worm" illustrates the precarious balance to be kept between public derision and admiration. Yet stardom they had reached, often before they actually starred in Tod Browning's Hollywood production. And despite the fact that *Freaks* was a financial disaster for MGM and was pulled early in its initial run, the reputation of its "stars" went on undamaged.

There is a 1941 photograph of a freak sideshow at the Vermont State Fair of September 1941. It was taken by Jack Delano, one of the famous documentary photographers who had gone out under government auspices to capture the face of the American nation as it lived, unbroken, through the years of the 1930s Great Depression. Most of the tens of thousands of photographs that came out of this official Farm Security Administration (FSA) project are in black and white. With the Kodachrome revolution of the late 1930s, though, some FSA photographers took up the new technique and bathed their pictures of a resurgent America in saturated sumptuous color. Delano's photograph captured a touring freak sideshow announcing its attractions on colorful billboards, posted side by side. It culminated in the proud announcement that "Here, in person, are Zip and Pip," a reference to two so-called pinheads, microcephalics, that had appeared in Browning's film. In all likelihood it falsely appropriated a name that had been famous in the sideshow world since the late 1800s. It testified to the star quality that many freaks had acquired among the larger public. Yet at the same time it hid the story of the fate that had befallen many freaks in the preceding years. They had drawn the attention of the medical community and its early views of disabled bodies as somehow subhuman, as genetically degenerate, a biological throwback to earlier stages of development of the human race. Many freaks in the 1930s with mental retardation were no longer seen as proper agents of public entertainment. They were removed from the public gaze and put in mental institutions.

One specific angle in this medicalization of the perception of freaks was the point of view of eugenics, which conceived of them as a threat to the healthy body of the nation. America, in the 1920s and '30s, had moved into an era in which seeing real people with disabilities out in public space was no longer acceptable; it had become an affront to the "moral order of the body" and the curative power of science and medicine. From the late 1860s to the 1970s, so-called ugly laws had been adopted in a number of American cities meant to keep disabled people from public view.[3] Freaks should no longer be seen as "celebrities," but as abnormal humans who needed to be hidden in institutions rather than displayed. A strategic role in this reconceptualization of the freak from a eugenics perspective was played by the Eugenics Record Office (ERO), set up in 1910 on Long Island, New York, under the direction of leading eugenicist Charles Davenport. Scientists from the ERO made special trips to the entertainment center on Coney Island, which included amusement parks and human spectacle presentations—that is, freak shows. There they took photographs and collected information on sideshow performers. These performers may have been curious spectacles for the crowds, but the eugenicists saw their disabilities as bad heredity. Davenport began observing freak shows for specimens in his scientific theories. With their reports and photographs, the ERO hoped to eliminate deviant bodies to "normalize" the population of the United States. This ominous project came to an end after the Carnegie Institution withdrew all funding following a review of the office's work. Their reports and articles have since been discredited, and were no longer considered to present scientific facts.[4]

It is true that American scientists and moralists were tough on the freak show, but their approach to oppression never went beyond disseminating their views and promoting legislation. Sideshows, traveling or stationary, went on to entertain the masses. Freaks went on to inform the public themselves through the production under their own auspices of so-called *cartes de visite*, as they had done since the mid-nineteenth century. Human "prodigies" had carefully posed photographs taken and often ordered thousands of reproductions. They would sometimes write about themselves on the back of the card, bragging about their physical attributes or talents. These *cartes de visite* were widely collected by Americans and made quite a bit of money for the freaks and the owners of freak shows. Freaks, in all such cases, kept a measure of control as the agent of their own public persona.

How different a course their lives had taken in America compared with developments in Europe. How lucky midgets Hans and Frieda could count themselves, both emigres from Germany at the time of World War I. A whiff of Germanness had never left them in their theatrical performance, in tribute to American vaudeville's stock German characters. Their language is strangely German in idiom and evokes a world of German aristocracy and social manners, a world also of Lilliput towns that had provided safe havens for midgets to lead their lives as they chose to, yet were open to the public. Like Hans and Frieda themselves, the idea of Lilliput towns had crossed the Atlantic and become a feature of the entertainment on offer at Coney Island, known as Lilliputia, resembling, at half-scale, fifteenth-century Nuremberg, Germany.⁵ But the country that Hans and Frieda had left behind had cruelly changed behind their backs. After the Nazi takeover of power in 1933, the new government issued its "Law for the Prevention of Progeny with Hereditary Diseases." People with so-called hereditary illnesses had to be sterilized. In 1937, Germany passed a law making freak shows illegal, decrying them as exploitation, thus making it legal for the Nazis to arrest freak show acts and subject their members to Nazi-style sado-medical experiments. A well-known and poignant case is that of the Transylvanian Jewish Ovitz family, sent to Auschwitz on May 7, 1944. The family members all had dwarfism, an affliction technically known as pseudo-achondroplasia. They had previously traveled as a musical troupe. Nazi doctor Josef Mengele subjected them to his gruesome medical experiments, yet fascinated by their deformity also displayed them, stripped naked, to groups of senior Nazis while lecturing on their inferior genetics. He also created a film for Adolf Hitler's amusement starring the Ovitz family. If there is an echo here of Nuremberg, it is the Nuremberg of the anti-Jewish race laws aimed at preserving the purity of Germany's Aryan stock.

Here the lines of my following argument are beginning to fall into place. It is the synchronicity of forms of spectacle as they took place on both sides of the Atlantic in the 1920s and '30s that I wish to explore. Public spectacle, its audiences and central actors, are the template underlying the comparisons that I will make. The sideshow as it developed in American public entertainment has all the necessary ingredients: the spectators and the stage that draws their gaze, plus, crucially, the optical regime that draws an invisible line setting spectators apart from the subjects of their attention. It is a line, though, that can be transgressed by acts of empathy and imaginary identification, making for a community of feeling. On the other hand such a line can set apart and separate, define inclusion versus exclusion. Freaks, for instance, can either be jeered at as human worms, vermin, or seen as princes, worthy of respect and deference. Identities can thus be collectively constructed in intricate exchanges across the line of separation. Freaks can be made, human beings can be turned into freaks. And spectacles, as I conceive of them, are the productive settings for this to unfold.

In this vein I will be looking at spectacles in the United States beyond the traditional freak show, spectacles such as public lynchings, events that turned their victims into freaks, writhing as they were tortured to death, while the public looked on in morbid fascination.

As these witnesses must have seen it, a threat to the social body of their community was being stamped out. Changing context and focus, I will also be looking at the way that in the late 1930s in Germany Jewish citizens were herded together and paraded through the streets in acts of instant enfreakment, of physical othering, exposed to the howls and jeers of an agitated public.

If these are the dark scenarios, leading to exclusion and ostracism, if not physical annihilation, the common element connecting those who do the excluding and ostracizing is the anguished feeling of having suffered a contamination of their collective purity. If there are positive scenarios—and there are, as we will see—they consist in the creative and transgressive affiliation across lines of division as these present themselves. As the voice of the sideshow barker in the film *Freaks* reminds us: "But for the accident of birth, you might even be as they are."

Freak Shows, Spectacle, and Specularity

Freak shows have always been a form of entertainment. Their history as an organized institution dates back to the opening in New York of P. T. Barnum's first museum in 1841, yet the extraordinary, or grotesque, or monstrous human body (as it was variously called over time) had a long history of scrutiny and fascinated interpretation. It had always drawn the intrigued, if not bewildered, gaze of those who conformed more closely to the statistically normal. They may in embarrassment have looked askance, or, forming throngs, have hounded the grotesque outcast, throwing stones and abuse in endless, merciless replays of medieval painter Hieronymus Bosch's nightmarish evocations of the defamation of Christ. Such age-old carnivalesque mob scenes have always managed to find the freakish outsider as the necessary Other for the collective affirmation of community and normality. With Barnum, though, the mob was domesticated, transformed into a public contained by an optical regime including spectators as much as it did the freaks on display. The public, at the price of admission, was invited to enjoy the pleasures of human difference, physical or mental, or more precisely to satisfy their morbid fascination with the humanly abnormal, all safely contained within a panopticon setting, separating observers from the observed in a balance of power favoring the observer.[6] The public display of freaks was at the same time a strategy of containment, creating a distance between freaks and normal humans, and allaying fears that "there but for fortune stand you and I." As in zoos, the spectatorial arrangement created a distance for observation that could also serve as the space for reverie and fantasy, for imaginative exploration of borders and border crossings, for taking the role of the other, be it chimpanzee or freak. If there was the magnetic pull of the abyss on the other side, the optical regime was there to prevent people from succumbing to this spell. But as we may remember from Mikhail Bakhtin's explorations of carnivals and other border-crossing, or *transgressive*, occasions, societies have historically offered a range of options to pursue precisely such empathetic fantasies of exchanging identities.[7] The borderline between the devious and the straight is never rigid nor given, but subject to social construction and contestation, based on fiction rather than empirical fact. Due to the extraordinary powers of empathy that fiction holds over its readers, novels may well be the ideal instrument to teach us empathy with the weird and freakish. Thus, in his 2010 novel *The Third Reich,* Roberto Bolaño has a scene on a tourist beach on the Costa Brava in Spain. Two couples on the beach observe a man who rents out pedal boats. As he emerges from the water having launched one of his boats, the onlookers see the burns covering most of his face, neck, and chest, dark and corrugated. They convince themselves that nobody is born like that. The burns weren't recent. "They probably dated back five years, or even more to judge by the attitude of the poor guy . . . , who had clearly grown used to attracting the same interest and stares as monsters and the mutilated, glances of involuntary revulsion, of pity at a great misfortune. To lose an arm or a leg is to lose a part of oneself, but to be burned like that is to be transformed, to become someone else."[8] As if in Barnum's museum, the onlookers weigh options, interpret what they see, and wonder whether this is a birth defect or the effect of an accident. In this vignette of curiosity, empathy, and fantasy, the typical freak's public is captured beautifully, to the point of its wondering about the aspect of transformation, of "becoming someone else."

There is one element missing in this particular vignette, an element that forms the gripping, if not haunting, quality to so many of these cross-border encounters, the element of eye contact, the exchange of glances. They are often experienced and told in words suggestive of a hint of understanding, a feeling of rapport. Toward the end of William Faulkner's *Light in August,* there is a lynching.[9] The atrocities are mostly suggested, not explicitly described. Seen through the eyes of members of the lynching pack, the reader is given to understand what the leader of the pack, Grimm, has been doing to the victim. "When they saw what Grimm was doing one of the men gave a choked cry and stumbled back into the wall and began to vomit. Then Grimm too sprang back, flinging behind him the bloody butcher knife. 'Now you'll let white women alone, even in hell,' he said." The deed has been done, a castration has been perpetrated. The victim is left to bleed to death. "The man on the floor had not moved. He just lay there, with his eyes open and empty of everything save consciousness, and with something, a shadow, about his mouth. For a long moment he looked up at them with peaceful and unfathomable and unbearable eyes." As the blood rushed out of his loins "like the rush of sparks from a rising rocket," in what is described as a last "black blast" (are we to understand this as a metaphor, an image of a last victorious and retaliatory ejaculation?), "the man seemed to be soaring into their memories forever and ever." If seeds had been planted, they were the seeds of ineradicable memory.

By 1932, when Faulkner published *Light in August*, white Southerners had perpetrated thousands of lynchings. Yet Faulkner, according to his own account, had never witnessed a lynching. He must have read about them, and heard stories told. In his creative reworking of these elements, he reconceptualized them through powers of imagination and empathy that emphasize the present as simply a moment in the long chain of memory. Central to his account of the final transfixed gaze of lynchers witnessing the dying moments of their victim is the instant translation into the long life of memory. This may be characteristic of Faulkner's more general attitude toward the present, seen as only the most recent chink in a longer chain of memory. Yet it may also help us understand the magic transactions taking place in the brief moments of an exchange of glances, moments of transgression, establishing through eye contact rapport and empathy across dividing lines separating insiders from outsiders, the established from those beyond the pale. Whatever the precise dividing line, there is always that no-man's-land on either side of the line that only the human imagination can straddle. It is a liminal space where fantasy is given free rein, as in the case when a child in the zoo taps on the glass to draw the attention of the gorilla behind it, or when King Kong and the woman protagonist in the various film versions of the story exchange glances suggestive of a sentimental bond forming. There is the brief, but unforgettable moment toward the end of Tod Browning's *Freaks*, when the freaks take terrible revenge on Cleopatra. The revenge posse is led by a freak without arms or legs, Prince Randian, also known as the Human Worm. As he is squirming to move forward through the mud, three seconds into the close-up, Randian breaks the "fourth wall," briefly escaping the narrative as he looks directly into the camera. It is the only time this is allowed to happen in the film. While used to being the object of the gaze of others, Randian now returns the gaze and takes command of its direction, upsetting the conventional balance of power in the world of the freak sideshow.

This reference to *Freaks* may give us pause to reflect on early twentieth-century changes in the public exposure to freaks and everything they represented in terms of the grotesque, the macabre, the shock caused by physical deformities and disfigurement. For one thing, in the wake of World War I human wreckage had washed across public space, with people maimed and mutilated an unavoidable presence. Their gruesome features found reflection in artists' representations, most directly in German painting by Max Beckmann or George Grosz, and more indirectly in the visual horror we may recognize in German cinema of the time, with its expressionist evocations of the macabre and horrendous in films like Robert Wiene's 1920 horror film *The Cabinet of Dr. Caligari*, Friedrich W. Murnau's 1922 *Nosferatu*, or, from the same year, Fritz Lang's *Dr. Mabuse, The Gambler*. Altogether different sources were tapped to cater for this general appetite for the freakish and grotesque as were to be found in the work of French author Victor Hugo, a towering figure in nineteenth-century French cultural and political life. His huge novels, broad allegories of noble impulses toward fairness and freedom doing battle with forces of repression and iniquity, were like tales of ultimate redemption following terrible tribulations. Good may come out victoriously in the end, but often in highly symbolic ways, in a transcendence of the common worldly course of events. Epic tales like *The Hunchback of Notre Dame*, with the haunting figure of Quasimodo, or *Les Misérables*, were given cinematic renditions; the former was turned into a hugely successful Hollywood film in 1923, while at least ten film versions of the latter came out between 1906 and 1925, four of which were American. Together they had established the mass appeal of Hugo's stories before his last and perhaps greatest novel—*L'homme qui rit* (The Man Who Laughs)—was brought to the screen in 1928. In this film we see the convergence of a number of developments crucially important for the public representation of freakishness. The first and most important is the rise of film itself as a medium turning the traditional traveling freak show into a mass spectacle. Never before had so many been able to indulge their morbid fascinations or, in the dark of movie theaters, to engage in fantasies of identification and empathy with freaks. A second crucial confluence occurring in these years was not only the transatlantic adoption of separate European strands of imagination of the macabre and grotesque but also the fact that a great number of European artists, actors, directors, writers, and composers had converged on Hollywood. Thus, *The Man Who Laughs* had a German director, Paul Leni, who had won acclaim as a leading figure in German expressionist cinema with, for example, *Das Wachsfigurenkabinet* (The Cabinet of Wax Figures). The lead actor also was German, Conrad Veidt, remembered for his role in *The Cabinet of Dr. Caligari.*[10] Now, in *The Man Who Laughs*, he impersonated Hugo's central tragic character of Gwynplaine, son of an English peer of the realm who had incurred the wrath of the English king and was sent into exile. The son, at an early age, was sold to a roving band of kidnappers, the Comprachicos, who cruelly disfigured his face, turning it into a freakish mask with an indelible grimace running from ear to ear. His inner emotional life had been forever sundered from the inane frozen grimace, inviting laughter and hilarity, if not abhorrence, among all those whose eyes beheld him. Yet, in a master stroke of creative genius, Hugo had paired this tragic victim of mutilation to an angelic, almost ethereal, blind girl, Déa, whose power of inner vision allowed her to see Gwynplaine unblemished, in the

full beauty of his inner person. If, at the end of the story, they
are bound in eternal union, it is not on this earth but in heaven.

There is a transcendent lesson in Hugo's vision of the human
power to look beyond the face of human appearance in search
of an inner and deeper humanity, a lesson for all those who are
confronted with deformed and disfigured fellow human beings.
But there are more lessons to be learned, lessons to do with the
power of human agency on this earth rather than the hereafter.
At one climactic moment in the story, Gwynplaine, restored to
what is rightfully his, the status of a peer of the realm, addresses
a full session of the House of Lords. Through a superhuman ex-
ertion of will, he manages to control the frozen expression of
his mask and to capture the attention of those in attendance.
He speaks, as he puts it, on behalf of all those downtrodden
masses of mankind, kept down by the tyrannical system of a
handful lording it over the rest of society. It is not long, though,
before the contagious grimace takes over and the House breaks
out in hilarious fracas, rolling about with laughter. Gwynplaine
is literally laughed out of court, his message lost to those whom
it concerned. This, probably, is the central tragic vignette of the
quandary of all those imprisoned behind a mask, a physical ex-
terior, not of their own choosing or making. Yet, if agency, if will
power, was thwarted in Gwynplaine's case, it helps us recognize
those moments where the struggle ends in victory. I, for one, was
reminded of these moving words by James Baldwin, from his
last interview. He too had known a struggle to overcome the
restraints of a mask; being black, being gay, with a face that was
not everyone's idea of male beauty, he bore a visual stigma that
the outside world responded to before it took pains to know his
inner self. This is what he had to say: "My father taught me . . .
what to fight for. At first I was only fighting for safety, or money.
Then I fought to make you look at me. Because I was not born
to be what someone said I was. I was not born to be defined by
someone else, but by myself, and myself only."[11]

"Then I fought to make you look at me." These words by

James Baldwin take us back to our earlier reflections on the gaze in the interactions between freaks and their observers. Reflections like these may remind us of Alan Trachtenberg's chapter on illustrious Americans in his *Reading American Photographs*.[12] Having introduced the reader to the early ways of exhibiting photographs of leading citizens in the established tradition of the picture gallery, confirming and reasserting social hierarchies, he turns the tables and looks at a collection of slave photographs, giving them the same close and careful attention as he gives the gallery-type pictures. The photographs—daguerreotypes—were made at the behest of celebrated Harvard natural scientist Louis Agassiz by J. T. Zealy, a local daguerreotypist in South Carolina. They were intended as anthropological specimens, to illustrate racial characteristics. The sitters, stripped of their clothes, had been turned into mere objects to the cold scientific gaze. Their humanity taken from them, they were made to represent bodily types in mid-nineteenth century natural science reflections on the possible polygenesis of varieties of humankind. In his passage on these slave photographs, Trachtenberg has this to say: "Without a public mask to mediate their encounter with the lens, the eyes of the enslaved Africans can only reveal the depths of their being—for, as naked slaves, they are permitted no social persona. . . . The Zealy pictures reveal the social convention which ranks blacks as inferior beings, which violates civilized decorum, which strips men and women of the right to cover their genitalia. And yet the pictures shatter that mold by allowing the eyes of [the sitters] to speak directly to ours, in an appeal to a shared humanity. This represents an extraordinary achievement, partly Zealy's (the photographer), partly due to the marvel of photography itself" (p. 56). The daguerreotypes are so compelling because in spite of the coerciveness they represent, they possess a power of communication greater than the likenesses of posturing civic leaders in photography galleries in New York.

This power of photographed people to stare back, to cast a meaningful glance, inviting our attention, is what Marianne

Hirsch, in her *The Familial Gaze*, has called the specularity—
from Latin *speculum*, "mirror"—of photographic portraits, looking at us yet mirroring our gaze and making for an mutuality of
glances.[13] She points to the element of exchange between the gaze
captured in a photograph and the eye of the observer. Meaning
is being read into the expression of the gaze in the photograph.
Yet, unlike exchanges in real life, before a photograph our specu-
lations on what is being "said," are one-sided, producing dialogues
in our heads rather than conversations with live people. In the case
of people long dead, particularly those we might never have met
in real life, like Zealy's black slaves, we can feel a chasm opening
up inside us, an abyss that not even the magic of glances locked
in exchange can bridge. Those on the other side of the abyss gaze
at you and beckon to you, clamoring for your attention, like the
shades of the dead calling to Odysseus during his visit to Hades,
or the figures speaking to Dante in the *Divine Comedy*. Yet such
urgent declarations of self and calls for recognition leave the living in impotent melancholy.

No single image captures this feeling, this mixture of melancholy and the nostalgia of farewell, quite as well as Edward
Curtis's famous 1904 picture entitled "The Vanishing Race." All
of Curtis's work in the photography of American Indians can
be seen as a tribute to their cultural heritage on the eve of their
imminent extinction, inspired by a fatalistic sense of the course
of history, if not the course of American empire. The photograph,
I may remind the reader, shows five Indians on horseback riding
off toward a dark horizon. The fourth in line turns around on
the saddle and casts a glance back at the photographer, at us.
Captured in that wistful pose, he seems to bid farewell forever.
And the photograph's caption will forever set the reading of the
image for the observer whose single response to the Indian's gaze
can only be one of sorrow and nostalgia. If the Indians' time
in history as their own free agents was assumed to be up, they
were given a new lease on life as their own simulacrum, "free"
to reenact their lives on stage and on screen, as spectacle and en-

tertainment to satisfy the modern mass public's appetite for the exotic and extraordinary.

Parades: Festive and Vicious

Two points in time to set the parameters for this section:

1901: The Barnum and Bailey circus comes to the Netherlands. Four trains composed of sixty-seven specialized carriages took the entire caravan from one city to the next. The largest of a total of seventeen tents allowed for two shows a day which twelve thousand visitors could attend. Among the many fabulous items on the program was a display of human freaks. As the description in the program booklet had it: "The rarest of human beings on earth were there for all to see." The text went on to say: "These human specimens have the same sensations and feelings as other humans." The program also makes clear what freaks are, but adds that freaks themselves prefer to be known as prodigies, or human curiosities.

1930s in Europe: Many small people, dwarfs or Liliputteans, under special Nazi eugenicist programs were sterilized and/or killed under euthanasia programs until 1945. The view of freaks of nature here is one that sees them as "Untermenschen," degenerates, unworthy of procreation or even a normal life.

The first view emphasizes the common humanity that human prodigies and normal people share. It is the view expressed in the first motto to this text, a quotation from Montaigne. It invites audiences to empathize, and to translate their curiosity into interaction, starting conversations, buying *cartes de visite* from freaks. P. T. Barnum, as the master impresario of impression management, constantly played games at the borderlines of the optical regimes that traditionally set audiences apart from people put on display. He invited the public as it were to see for themselves and not believe what he told them, to engage in an exchange of meaningful glances between observers and observed. Photographs, such as *cartes de visite*, allowed people to return to those moments of exchange and to continue an inner conversation with people physically different, visibly Other. Thus in the display of freaks, many have been the instances of a mediating gaze, turning otherness and difference into an invitation to empathize with freaks as fellow humans. The gaze may have come directly from the freaks themselves, inviting the public to acknowledge their gaze and respond to it, or through the work of sympathetic intermediaries such as film makers and photographers. The optical regime, of the panopticum as in the freak show, or set by the framing of the cinema screen or the photograph, made for borderlines that invited playful transgression. If borderlines had been drawn, it was to set the playing field for these games of exchange and empathy to be played, and for fantasies of individual identities blurring to be indulged. Diane Arbus may have had this in mind when she gave an account of her work, a body of photography of arresting, absorbing images of dwarfs, twins, giants, nudists, and carnies: "I really believe there are things which nobody would see unless I photographed them."[14] Together with other artists expanding the boundaries of photography in the 1960s, she altered the way we understand portraiture and thus the way we see people. She was criticized, most notably by Susan Sontag, for providing the cheap thrills of gazing at freaks. She was applauded by others for turning the idea of the outsider into a compelling investigation of the possibilities and limits of representing otherness. Her images stopped us in our tracks and stayed in our minds.

Yet the freedoms of constructionism implied here, of identities being open to revamping and recasting, may sensitize us to two further implications. For one thing, as Robert Bogdan emphasized in his *Freak Show*, and again more recently in his *Picturing Disability*, freaks as a category are a matter of social construction.[15] Freaks were made, manufactured, to fit certain modes of presentation dictated by the amusement world. The defining lines are therefore relatively open and fluid and can change over time. Thus, in May 1971, at the Mayday demonstrations in Washington, DC, at one of the largest actions of civil disobedience in U.S. history, many of the thousands gathered now called themselves "freaks." Speaking to their emerging collective power, activist Frank Hammer addressed the crowd, shouting, "Twenty thousand freaks carry the seeds now, and they have been blown to every corner of the land."[16] Clearly, by the early 1970s, the meaning of "freak" had been reinscribed in American culture. What had once been a pejorative used to single out and mark corporeal difference and delineate the lines of the "normal citizen" was now embraced as a term of choice.

If freak then is a label that one can choose to adopt as a nom de guerre in antinomian social movements, at the same time it can make for strategies of ostracism, projecting the label onto groups that people wish to put outside the bounds of shared community. These are the two implications I referred to above, the one implying a festive inclusion in a self-styled community of freaks, breaking the oppressive hold of imposed social categories, the other implying a vicious exclusionary strategy, turning groups into social outcasts, as alien, and unassimilable Others. Again, the film *Freaks* grippingly illustrates this duality. Toward the end of the film, during the banquet in celebration of the wedding between trapeze artist Cleopatra and her midget man Hans, the collected freaks around the table welcome Cleopatra into their midst with a pounding "One of Us, One of Us, We Accept Her, We Accept Her." In horror and disgust Cleopatra shouts back "Freaks! Freaks! Filthy, slimy FREAKS!" Having rejected her honorary inclusion into the community of freaks, they retaliate by excommunicating her, not only from their midst but also from human society. She can no longer return to normal humanity following the horrific revenge of the freaks. They leave her mutilated and maimed, altered into a chicken woman, the freak that she had refused to become. Excommunication is presented here in the classic freak mode, as spectacle, turning Cleo into a spectacular body ready to be put on display.[17]

This is a point that I wish further to elaborate in the final part of my argument. If freaks traditionally have found their place in social and cultural rituals and constructions, these always included the setting and context for their display in front of an audience. Thus, when the circus came to town, there was the parade down Main Street, with the animals, the clowns, and freaks whetting the appetites of the public. The local population walked along with the circus train, in exhilaration and anticipation of the spectacle to come. There was an unspoken stage direction that all involved knew and followed. It contained the forces of carnivalesque joy, keeping them within bounds known to all involved.

Similar conventions applied when the occasion was not one of *welcoming* spectacular Others, but of setting them apart, ostracizing them. The parades in these instances were spectacles of eviction, exorcising forces of evil that had intruded into the social body of the community. If there was an unspoken stage direction here it was one aimed at restoring the healthy life of the community in a public display of the intrusive elements of contagion and corruption. In a masterful study of lynching rituals in the American South, rightly called *Lynching and Spectacle*, Amy Louise Wood analyses the long history of this sad practice.[18] With an uncanny empathy she sets out to understand the collective emotions shared by the lynching mob. Lynching was not simply the extralegal killing of those who had trespassed, who had broken social and legal rules. Sometimes it was just that, a quick settling of scores outside the public view. But more often the social response assumed the form of the gruesome theater of revenge, of a ritual restoring the ruptured texture of communal life, meting out punishment and revenge on the perpetrator of the crime. Crucially the crime was one of sexual transgression, by a black man soiling the purity of white womanhood. The atavistic fears were always of impure blood getting mixed with that of white people, of the gene pool of whites being polluted by beings closer to animals than to humans. In public rituals of what

Large crowd looking at the burned body of Jesse Washington,
eighteen-year-old African American, lynched in Waco, Texas, May 15,
1916. *Library of Congress.*

one might call the eugenics of the mob, lynching victims were not
only killed in atrocious ways, tortured, hanged, burned. Tellingly,
they were often castrated and left to hang as a warning to others.
One of the more disturbing features of this theater of revenge
were the uses made of the modern invention of photography. All
the noises of mob action have gone from the photographs. In
many of them the crowd has regrouped in almost solemn witness
to the act of vengeful retaliation, as if to bring across the point
that justice had been done, and the purity of the "body social"
had been defended.[19]

The photographs were widely distributed, kept in memory
of the spectacle, sent to friends and relatives as postcards. They
elicited the morbid fascination with the lynching spectacle, with
bodies hanging in strangely contorted poses, or with the charred
remains of lynching victims. If the initial response to these photographs was one of reaffirmation of Southern ways of justice,

as they spread across the country and were even beginning to be published in the black press, they became tools in the hands of antilynching activists, of people with different views of the inclusiveness of humanity. Lynching photographs spread as far as countries in Europe and affected European views of America. One early example are the travel reports by a German socialist, Arthur Holitscher, published in separate installments in *Die neue Rundschau* in 1911 and as a book in 1912, entitled *Amerika heute und morgen* (America Today and Tomorrow). He went in depth into the lawless conditions of life of the Negro population in the American South, illustrating his argument with a photograph "Idyll from Oklahama" [*sic*]; it showed two lynched blacks hanging from trees, with a group of white men facing the camera. The cynical tone of the caption will not have escaped the readers, among whom was a budding author, Franz Kafka. In the sketches for his unfinished novel, published as *Amerika*, Kafka gives his white protagonist, Karl Rossman, the nickname "Negro" and sends him to Oklahama (using the misspelling from the photograph's caption).[20]

Lynching photographs made Europeans aware of the disheartening idylls that America invented. But it was not long before Europe came up with its own obscene rituals. From the 1930s on, similar uses were made of spectacles and parades as strategies of eviction, branding people as unworthy members of the community. Not only did they affect communities of freaks, defining them on eugenicist grounds as unworthy of procreation and a threat to the healthy life of the "normal" community. Also, following the Nazi takeover of political power, rules of social inclusion or exclusion were overhauled, defining new threats to the purity of the German *Volk*. As in the American South, the rituals of expulsion, of redefinitions of Them versus Us, used the same repertoire of parades and public spectacles to set established sections of the community apart as "freaks of nature," as people of different genetic heredity. As this campaign gathered force, it culminated in the infamous "Kristallnacht" in 1938, a night of destruction of synagogues and Jewish-owned shops, as well as of regular progroms. In a number of German small towns members of the established Jewish bourgeoisie were rounded up and paraded through the streets. What photographs can still show us today is the exhilaration evoked by the act of social ostracizing among the throngs of people walking along with the parade, jeering at those being paraded. One can't help being reminded of so many other episodes of people being paraded before hissing crowds, being turned into inassimilable freaks, in lynching photographs, or in pictures of black students being escorted to school in the late 1950s, surrounded by angry crowds.

One such moment of Jews being paraded, being instantly turned into Others, open to public defamation and abuse, is captured in photographs taken in Oldenburg on the day following "Kristallnacht." Some are reprinted in a book by a descendant of one of the people "on parade."²¹ Dignified in the midst of so much public hysteria, one of the Jewish citizens, a well-dressed bourgeois gentleman looks from the picture into our eyes. He establishes eye contact across the divide of time, but more poignantly across the abyss opening up in Germany at the time. He thus makes the viewer more acutely aware of the human drama unfolding before our eyes.

There were those at the time who pointed to the similarities of what was happening in the American South and in Nazi Germany. Remarkably, a Jewish scholar from Germany, Kurt Baschwitz, who had found refuge in the Netherlands, saw the historical parallels and the logic behind it. In what would become a classic study in mass psychology, published in exile in Amsterdam, the author saw his analysis of processes of mob behavior confirmed in both settings, in an amazing act of creating intellectual distance to current events even as they had such immediate dramatic relevance to his own life.²² Famous film director Fritz Lang, another refugee from Nazi Germany, made much the same point when he was shooting *Fury*, his 1936 Hollywood film on lynching and lynching mobs. In a 1936 interview, for instance, he

Jewish men rounded up and paraded through the town of Oldenburg. *By permission of Arbeitskreis Erinnerungsgang Oldenburg.*

Mass arrest of Jewish men, Oldenburg, November 9, 1938. *Photo, The Wiener Library, London.*

Oldenburg mass arrest of Jewish citizens, 1938. *By permission of the United States Holocaust Memorial Museum.*

Jewish men paraded through Oldenburg, to the merriment of at least some bystanders. *By permission of Bildagentur BPK, Berlin.*

recalled his own encounters with mob mentality growing up in
Vienna along the Russian front, fighting in World War I, and, of
course, working in Berlin as Hitler came to power.[23]

The worst atrocities were yet to come, and photography
would be there to document the perpetrators in their acts. One
example that I will mention in conclusion is the infamous Stroop
report, a collection of photographs taken in the Warsaw Ghetto
in 1943. German SS troops were busy quashing the Warsaw
Ghetto uprising. Jürgen Stroop, commanding officer in charge
of the operation, had the photographs taken to be collected in a
scrapbook, titled "The Jewish Quarter of Warsaw Is No More!"
He donated it to his boss, Heinrich Himmler, as testimony to
a mission accomplished. The images are properly to be seen as
trophy photographs in a construction of the victims, *not* as worthy human opponents, but as vermin to be smoked out ("fumi-
gated," as the caption to one photograph has it) and recast in the
photographs as freaks, as grotesque deformities. This of course
was fully in line with established modes of Nazi propaganda,
which notoriously represented Jews as freakish monsters. One
photograph in particular is included, we must assume, to corrob-
orate this reading, a photograph of two naked men: seen from
behind, one utterly deformed by scoliosis, his vertebral column
twisted into an S-shape. The caption simply says: "Abschaum der
Menschheit," dregs of humanity.[24]

Some of the other photographs show the way that Jews,
emerging from their hiding places, were marched off under the
watchful eyes of SS personnel, "paraded," so to speak, before the
camera, on their way to the gathering spot for transportation
to the concentration camp. They are unforgettable photographs.
Like lynching photographs they were ultimately turned against
their makers and used as proof of inhumanity at the Nurnberg
trials. They were later on selected by Edward Steichen for *The
Family of Man*, a photo show seen by millions all over the Cold
War world, in his attempt to embrace all of humanity in a familial gaze, and to re-create a reading of humanity that gave central

emphasis to inclusion, not exclusion. The photographs of Jews being herded on their way to extinction even today allow of vicarious participation. One photograph in particular has acquired an iconic power that turns it into *the* visual representation of the Holocaust. One fragment of the photograph especially has assumed a life of its own, the image of a boy, forlorn and terrified, his hands raised. He calls forth feelings of pity and impotence in the viewer, an effect so strong that even a student of photography such as Barbie Zelizer misremembers the photograph. As she describes it the boy is looking us in the eye.[25] This must be wishful thinking on her part. The boy's eyes are bewildered, expressive of fear, but focused on nothing in particular. The boy is forever beyond our fantasy of establishing rapport. The photograph in which he features so prominently has acquired an afterlife of its own, as a document of transgression of the thin line separating humanism from barbarism. It will come back to haunt us in the following chapter.

AMERICAN RESPONSES TO THE HOLOCAUST:
ATROCITY PHOTOGRAPHS AS NOMADIC OBJECTS

THIS IS A tale of three photographs. Or more precisely, a tale of
their afterlife as nomadic objects. What they have in common is
that each relates to the Holocaust. The first photograph that we
shall be looking at more closely below forms part of the body of
photographs taken at the time that the Allied forces reached the
Nazi concentration camps. They document the atrocity of what had
taken place in those camps in faithful execution of Nazi policies of
racial extermination. Photo journals like *Life* published many of
the atrocity photographs, turning stunned audiences in the United
States into secondary, or vicarious, witnesses of the inconceivable evil
of Nazism. The other two were taken by the perpetrators or at least
were commissioned by them. They belong to the genre of trophies
to be shown as proof of the "good" work done for the Nazi cause.

The three photographs that will occupy us here have one
further element in common. Diverse as their origins may be, as
well as the history of their public exposure—the trajectory, in
other words, of their photographic afterlife—they now share a
common status as iconic images. They find general recognition;
people remember having seen them before. But if they have become icons, the question arises: icons of what? If they have come
to represent something more abstract and general, such as the
Holocaust, or the Shoah, what, in their elevation to this status,

have they lost in terms of the specific historical moment that they illustrate and capture? A further pressing question presents itself: what happened on the way from moment of origin to ultimate emblem during an afterlife that can truly be seen as that of a nomadic object, available to anyone interested in using and re-using it, without coordination, counsel, or guidance? What rival narratives and readings attached themselves to the images? How do these compare in terms of their truthfulness? Whose truths do they speak of? And perhaps most important, how do differences in the reading of these and similar photographs relate to differences in the context and setting of reception? Does it make a difference when these photographs originating in Europe and documenting European atrocities circulate in settings half a world away, in an America that had been spared the dilemma of being on the side of Nazism or at the receiving end of its evil schemes?

Photo I—George Rodger

This photograph was taken near concentration camp Bergen Belsen by British photojournalist George Rodger, on assignment for *Life* magazine, shortly after the camp had been liberated. He took the photograph on April 20, 1945, as one of a total of thirty-four taken at Bergen. It was first published in *Life* on May 7, 1945, the day Germany capitulated and World War II officially came to its end. The photograph introduced a cover story on "The German People." It carried the caption that the photographer had given it: "A small boy strolls down a road lined with dead bodies near camp at Belsen." On the page facing the photograph with the small boy the meaning of Bergen Belsen and another Nazi concentration camp, Buchenwald, gets more extensive visual treatment, with photographs of dying men and women, of starving people packed in triple-decker beds, and of emaciated bodies of prisoners. The image with the little boy—the only one given a full page by the editors—opened the photo essay with the title "Atrocities: Capture of the German Concentration

Young boy walks down dirt road, lined with the corpses of people
who died at Bergen-Belsen concentration camp. *George Rodger,
photographer. GettyImages.*

Camps Piles up Evidence of Barbarism that Reaches the Low
Point of Human Degradation" (shortened in the table of con-
tents to "German Atrocities"). Thus it came to form part of the
harrowing photojournalism that surrounded the liberation of
concentration camps more broadly, exposing the American public to a veritable flood of atrocity images. Yet *Life*'s photographic
documentation was double-edged. Its cover story on "The German People" also showed German children, thus setting a context for divergent readings of the photograph of the little boy.
Relatively well-dressed, not emaciated, averting his gaze—or so

it may have seemed[1]—from the rows of dead bodies, could he be a German boy, a typical representative of the ordinary, average Germans, an uncaring witness to the gruesome results of a reign of terror? For indeed, such was the gist of much photojournalism at the time, in compilations by Margaret Bourke-White and Lee Miller, among others, making the point that "Germans Are Like This," the title to Lee Miller's June 1945 reportage for *Vogue*, conflating Nazis and Germans into one, larger anti-German picture. Rodger's photograph could thus be seen as a specimen of the larger category of "images of witnessing," a separate genre of atrocity representation. Witnessing itself was depicted from various angles and perspectives, with the press initially featuring photos of official delegations, of members of Congress, of American editors, of General Eisenhower and other officers examining corpses at a concentration camp site near Ohrdruf. German nationals were also frequently depicted, German perpetrators as well as civilians. These latter, too, were photographed in various encounters with the atrocities: reburying the bodies of Nazi victims, looking at cremation ovens, or being forced to gaze at stacks of corpses. In her analysis of this particular category of atrocity photographs Barbie Zelizer makes the point that most shots of German civilians seemed to pronounce a confusion, shock, or bewilderment that complicated the act of bearing witness, as when German children were portrayed in a refusal to bear witness. She goes on to say: "One shot showed a small boy looking straight at the camera and away from the bodies that took up the majority of photographic space, his glance communicating an act of witnessing that was in essence not-witnessing; in another photo a boy walked down a road lined with dead bodies in Belsen, his head too averted—again, a refusal to bear witness."[2] She does not show the latter photograph, nor does she refer explicitly to its maker. Yet her description of it uncannily fits Rodger's photograph, which occupies us here. Together with many other photographs of the camps, particularly of Germans as bewildered or unwilling witnesses, Rodger's image could thus be incorporated as a contribution to an indictment of Germans, illustrating the point made above of all Germans being cast as equally callous and indifferent. Photography could become a form of accusation, and one trajectory in the afterlife of Rodger's photograph was in continuing connection to this accusatory reading. The photograph became an icon and was republished many times. A widely discussed recent history of the postwar period, Tony Judt's *Postwar*, opens its first picture insert with Rodger's photograph, accompanied by the following heading:

> Shortly after Germany's defeat in 1945, a child walks past the corpses of hundreds of former inmates of Bergen-Belsen concentration camp, laid out along a country road. Like most Germans in the post-war years, he averts his gaze.

This rather didactically guiding caption of the image appeared as late as 2005, a full sixty years after its taking. To this day similar captions accompany the photograph as it is accessible on various websites, including Getty Images (the heir to the copyright of *Life* magazine).

There is, however, a radically different way to read the photograph, which points to an afterlife going all the way back to its first publication in *Life*. As Werner Sollors tells the story, an uncle of the boy, who was living in New York, recognized his nephew in the photograph: Sieg Maandag, a Jewish boy from Amsterdam deported with his parents and younger sister via the Dutch transit camp of Westerbork to Bergen-Belsen. Yet it has taken years of research for this submerged afterlife of the picture to become public and restore the identity of the boy as a survivor, a victim of atrocity, not a typical representative of the Germans seen as bearing collective guilt or even as a nation of "willing executioners."[3]

Photo II

What we see here is a still from a film shot at Westerbork in 1944 by an inmate of the camp, a German Jewish cinematographer, at

Book cover, documentary about Settela. *By permission of author Aad Wagenaar and publisher Hans van Maar, Just Publishers.*

the behest of the German camp commander, SS Obersturmführer Albert Konrad Gemmeker. The film was meant to document the impeccable way he ran the camp with a view, one assumes, to impressing his superiors. The film was intended as a proud trophy in testimony to the good work he had done for the cause of National Socialism. Yet—and this may have been a brief moment of rebellion on the part of the film maker—alongside views of well-organized camp life, there is a seven-second glimpse of a girl looking out from a boxcar before the sliding door shuts her in on the way to extermination. Thus a haunting image was produced that came to represent the fate of so many deportees from the Netherlands, most of them Jews. In its afterlife it was used time and again, traveling across the world in documentary films about National Socialism and its concentration camps, films like French director Alain Resnais's *Nuit et Brouillard* (Night and Fog), premiered at the Cannes film festival in 1956.

In his 1965 classic study of the extermination of the Dutch

Jewish population, Dutch historian Jacob Presser, a Jew himself, refers to the film and to this fragment in particular. He wonders how it could have escaped SS commander Gemmeker that he had produced a powerful indictment of his doings. In fact, during his trial after the war the film fragment would be used against him. Presser goes on to say: "Whoever has seen the little girl, the helpless Jewish child, in terror before the doors slide shut, casting a last glance from the cattle car that is to take her toward an unknown destiny, will ask him- or herself the same question."

This reading of the photograph as an image of a young Jewish deportee has persisted to the present day. For example, in a program on Dutch television reconstructing the family history of Dutch Jewish novelist Leon de Winter (aired on February 20, 2011), the story of his parents' deportation from Westerbork is illustrated by this seven-second visual fragment, as a ready shorthand reference to the larger drama of Jewish deportation. Yet ever since the mid-1990s the true identity of the girl had been established through the tenacious research done by Dutch journalist Aad Wagenaar. In spite of many dead ends, unrelenting in his mission to establish the identity of the girl that he too, initially, had assumed to be Jewish, led him to the conclusion that here we had not a Jewish girl, but a Gypsy (or Roma) girl, representing a group in Dutch society that was as relentlessly persecuted as the Jews. As the subtitle to his book has it: "The girl has her name back," Settela. In fact, more than a name, a group identity. Thus, in the construction of the memory of the Holocaust, the Dutch Jews might have lost one icon, the forgotten group of Roma had gained one. It instilled among the larger public an awareness that not all trains leaving from Westerbork were deporting Jews toward their final destination, but that in fact one train might have been hiding another, as the sign at French railroad crossings keeps reminding us.

This larger view of what cargoes trains were carrying as they trundled through Nazi-occupied Europe forms a larger haunt-

One train hiding another. *Photograph by the author.*

ing memory image that for instance inspired American composer Steve Reich's masterpiece *Different Trains.* This composition stems from Reich's adult reflection that had he been a child in Europe in the 1940s, his fate might have been different: "As a Jew, I would have had to ride on very different trains."[4] Wagenaar's memory work was taken up by renowned Dutch documentary film maker Cherry Duyns, and given wider circulation via television.[5] Yet, as in the case of George Rodger's photograph, conflicting readings continue to exist side by side.

Photo III

Compared with the analysis of the two preceding photographs, our discussion of the third photograph will be more extensive. The image of "A child at gunpoint," as the photograph is often

Photo from the Stroop Report, *The Warsaw Ghetto Is No More.*

referred to, is another iconic emblem of the Holocaust. Like Settela, the Gypsy girl, this boy's photographic image originated in
the Nazi urge to document their doings; it had been a trophy
photograph before it became an iconic image of Nazi evil. Like
Settela's picture it set out on its worldwide circulation as a sym-
bol of Nazi atrocity through Resnais's 1956 film. And like so
many other nomadic photographs this photograph was taken
out of context, losing its historical specificity. In fact the boy
himself, in this recycling of his image, lost his identity. Again,
it was for meticulous historical research decades later to re-
construct the precise historical moment captured in this photograph. As the research has shown, the afterlife of this particular
photograph is particularly rich in resonance, accruing layer upon
layer of meaning and significance at the various stations of its
afterlife, an afterlife that more clearly than in the case of our previous two photographs proceeded on both sides of the Atlantic,
moving back and forth and never out of public sight or reference
for long.

In terms of its historical origin, what we have here is another instance of the use of photography to produce trophies to be sent to Nazi superiors as proof of work done to perfection. The photograph we see here was one of a series shot at the time of the final destruction of the Warsaw ghetto in the face of an uprising of the remaining Jewish population. The photographs formed part of a report prepared by the man in charge of the operation, SS General Jürgen Stroop. His leather-bound report bore the proud title: "Es gibt kein Jüdisches Wohnbezirk mehr in Warschau" (There Is No More Jewish Quarter in Warsaw). One copy, captured by American troops, was used at the Nurnberg trial as evidence of Nazi crimes. It was not until much later that the photograph of "The Child at Gunpoint," as it came to be titled, began its afterlife in various croppings, as an icon of Jewish resistance and heroism first, as an emblem of victimhood inflicted on innocent children later. The face of the child in the picture, with its bewildered expression, his hands raised, eventually found its recurrent use as a mnemonic device to call forth the larger image of the Holocaust in general.

Two historians in particular have taken it upon themselves to trace the afterlife of the photo and connect it back to the moment when it originated: Richard Raskin, in his book *A Child at Gunpoint: A Case Study in the Life of a Photo*, and Frédéric Rousseau, in his *L'enfant juif de Varsovie: Histoire d'une photographie*. The latter in particular has carefully reconstructed the Warsaw ghetto setting and the set of photographs included in the Stroop report. Both books offer a rich survey of what can happen to a photograph once it is put in the service of the larger mission of visualizing the Holocaust, of literally giving a face to it.[6]

Yet neither of them mentions a moment in the mass circulation and recycling of this particular image in the United States. Well before the large-scale recontextualization of the image took off in the 1960s and 1970s, the image had already been recombined with two others, one from the Stroop archive, the other taken in Israel in 1951, jointly displayed on a separate panel in

the section on "Man's Inhumanity to Man," for the famous 1955
exhibition of *The Family of Man*. Produced by Edward Steichen
for the Museum of Modern Art in New York, then bought by
USIA and sent touring the world as part of its Cold War cultural diplomacy efforts, the show was seen by millions. However,
given the central message of the show, that all of mankind was
one in the face of a new Holocaust, a nuclear one this time, the
reference to the recent history of atrocity in Europe was missed
by most viewers and reviewers, as later research has been able
to confirm.[7]

Only much later, in the mid-1990s, long after the show had
stopped touring, was it given a second lease of life. It was restored, reassembled, and put on permanent display in Luxembourg, birthplace of Edward Steichen. The occasion made for a
revisit of the show's inherent meanings and possible readings and
a repositioning of its place as a crucial public event in a world
that had emerged from World War II only to enter the apocalyp-
tic stage of the Cold War. New critical writing served to put the
show in this new historical perspective.[8] Furthermore, at the official opening of the show in its new home, a symposium brought
together an international group of historians with a view to a
critical revisit of the *Family of Man* in historical perspective.
Until that moment, all that had been available to the larger public to remind them of the show had been its catalog, which remarkably has never been out of print since the mid-1950s. Yet as
an archive to sustain people's memories of the show the catalog
poses major difficulties. For one thing, there are important differences between the arrangement of photographs in the catalog
and their order of display in the show. Crucially, for instance, the
only full-color transparency–of a nuclear mushroom forming–
was not in the catalog, although it was the show's single-image
carrier of its message of nuclear annihilation threatening all of
mankind. As for the show's reference to the Nazi holocaust, the
catalog contains some Warsaw ghetto images but does not reproduce the compelling order in which Streichen had put them

Family of Man Exhibition, Installation Shot, Clervaux, Luxembourg.
By permission of Centre National de l'Audiovisuel, Clervaux. © *CAN/
Romain, 2013.*

together on one of the show's separate panels. The photograph
of the boy with his hands raised is not in the catalog, nor did the
photograph of the Israeli woman have the same position as on
the panel in the show.

That may have been why the renewed confrontation with the

order of the photographs as originally intended by Steichen, and made possible by the show's reconstitution in Luxembourg, may have come as a shock. Rather than as a mere cultural relic, or a posthumous tribute to Steichen as its *auctor intellectualis*, eliciting nostalgia for its remembered meanings, the show proved it could go on and stimulate new readings. A notable collection of essays resulting from the Luxembourg symposium revisits the show in an acknowledgment of its continuing power to speak to current concerns and anxieties.[9] In one essay, Viktoria Schmidt-Linsenhoff engages the exhibit in terms not of its Cold War relevance but of what it has to say about the European trauma of the Holocaust, or the Shoah as she prefers to call it. When she reencountered the exhibit at Clervaux, Luxembourg, one picture with which she was familiar because of her earlier work on photography by the Nazi henchmen "took her breath away."[10]

Two photographs from the Stroop report on the destruction of the Warsaw ghetto—of groups of Jews marched off at gunpoint from the burning ghetto, one showing the little boy—were presented in such a way as to conceal and at the same time highlight the absence of the Shoah as the invisible center of the exhibition. In the two years of preparation for the original 1955 exhibit, Steichen must have gone over many of the concentration camp pictures that had circulated widely a mere eight years before. The photographs of Buchenwald, Dachau, and Bergen-Belsen were in the archives from which a majority of the material in the exhibition was taken. Yet, rather than include any of Lee Miller's photographs of heaps of corpses in Dachau, he selected Miller's moving image of a child and a cat as part of the closing section of the exhibition on children. Only one panel, in the section captioned "Man's Inhumanity to Man," may have served to trigger the visual archive of the unconscious in the minds of the show's visitors. Two photographs on that panel show men, women, and children being led at gunpoint out of the burning Warsaw ghetto on their way to the assembly point, the ominous

Umschlagplatz, before being herded by the Germans to their deaths in the Treblinka extermination camp. One of the two photographs, a little less prominently displayed than the other, shows the little boy, in its original full-frame version. A third photograph, at the right-hand top of the panel, was taken in Israel in 1951. It shows a black-haired woman in dark clothing, her emaciated arm raised aloft in a monumental gesture, the fingers eloquently splayed, in a spiritual cry of outrage. The configuration of photographs on the panel is meant to convey the impression that this woman is not only bewailing the suffering in the Warsaw ghetto but is triumphing over it. Centrally placed on the panel is a text quoted from George Sand: "Humanity is outraged in me and with me. We must not dissimulate nor try to forget this indignation which is one of the most passionate forms of love." Text and photographs together indicate that the image of the woman is an allegory of the state of Israel, a state whose origins lay in the suffering of innocent victims and which was retrospectively invested with the spirit and dignity of the founding sacrificial victims. Thus recontextualizing the images, Steichen imbues them with new meaning, connecting past trauma with future hopes. He did this at the same time that the young state of Israel was struggling to establish a meaningful connection between its national existence and the immediately preceding European history of the Holocaust. Steichen, though, may have had fewer qualms and anxieties about the imagery of Jewish victimhood than the Israeli authorities in their reading of the Holocaust. Particularly in the return to the Warsaw Ghetto uprising, Israel may initially have been more anxious—may indeed have felt a greater existential need—to see the image of heroic resistance, of Jewish combativity, in it than that of victimhood and surrender.[11]

Thus the *Family of Man* deals with the Shoah only through subtle recontextualization. Yet there are ways in which we can see Steichen's entire project as addressing issues of race and genocide. If, from one perspective, the exhibition can be considered the qualitative pinnacle of a stylistic genre known as human-interest photography, Steichen at the same time deconstructs the genre. As a genre, it had discovered the particular and the non-representative, the anecdotal. Steichen, though, chose to bend it toward his neohumanist purposes. He rhythmically punctuated the sequences of images of everyday life with archaic natural images of biblical force, obliterating the sensitivity to the "human interest" in the photographs. Thus, to quote Schmidt-Linsenhoff again: "This systematic inversion from the particular to the universal, from profane to sacred, from visual serendipity to divine plan for creation, clearly points to the horror unleashed by the 'senseless destruction of life for its own sake,' a horror which the exhibition addresses without showing the 'horrific images.'"[12] Steichen's entire vision can then be understood as one frantic attempt to send out a message of "Never Again." In the process the little, defenseless, boy in the picture unwittingly serves this larger purpose. If he raises his hands in surrender, we may see the gesture duplicated by the Israeli woman, not in defeat, but in victory. Steichen's gesture, in turn, can then be seen as an early instance of lifting the boy from his hopeless setting to the status of a messenger of hope.

Yet, in retrospect, when the *Family of Man* opened in New York in 1955, it may have been too early for the public to take in this more complex reading of Steichen's narrative. In spite of the exposure to atrocity photographs through mass circulation magazines like *Life* in the immediate postwar years, Americans may not have been sufficiently educated or sophisticated in reading Holocaust photographs, nor did they have the grasp of constructed meanings as these accrued later to these images, turning them into iconic representations. Steichen in fact made a remarkable authorial statement at the time by incorporating for public display atrocity photographs that had disappeared from mass public circulation in the United States and in Europe. Yet the true import of his vision has escaped many who have taken up the vexing question of the alleged public silence, on both sides of the Atlantic, on the traumatic recent history of the Shoah.[13]

Walking by Steichen's panels in the 1950s, people must have missed the triggering moments that later publics would unfailingly pick up. For one thing, the little boy's image in one of the two Warsaw Ghetto photographs had not yet acquired its iconic status. It would not have leapt at the viewer with the force it would gain later. Nor was Steichen out to educate the public and provide them with historical background. He wished the photographs in his assemblage to speak for themselves, weaving their voices together to tell stories as he envisaged them, irrespective of authorial intent of their makers. In the end, though, as the afterlife of *The Family of Man* may illustrate, not even Steichen's editorial command proved final and definitive. In its reception by viewers over the years, visiting and critically revisiting the show, the readings it was given proved unstable, inviting ever new narratives. If anything, the show had become as much a nomadic object as the many photographs that it brought together.

If, according to one such critical revisit on the occasion of the show's reopening in Luxembourg, we may now connect our contemporary recognition of the iconic "Child at Gunpoint" with the emblematic picture of the Israeli woman, it is only because in the meantime the Warsaw Ghetto child has undergone a long process of iconic construction. His image, in its afterlife as a nomadic object, continues to lend itself to the construction of narratives more instantly recognizable than at the time of Steichen's initial combination of photographic images. If it was Steichen's point at the time to construct a narrative connecting the Warsaw Ghetto images to the birth of Israel, we now see daring further steps along those lines.

In a work called "The Legacy of Abused Children from Poland to Palestine," Anglo-Israeli artist Alan Schechner, working and teaching in the United States, explores connections between the Holocaust and the Intifada. A born provocateur, he rubs many people the wrong way through his artistic interventions in history and memory.[14] Aware of the explosive potential of any connection made between the plight of European Jews at the

time of the Holocaust and that of Palestinians under Israeli occupation, the artist pointedly focuses attention on the suffering
of children rather than on supposed parallels between the SS and
Israeli soldiers. He imaginatively, and provocatively, combines a
cropped version of the Warsaw boy, showing the boy with hands
raised and the SS officer pointing his gun at him, with a Reuters
photograph of a Palestinian child being led away by a group of
Israeli soldiers, so terrified that he has wet his pants. In Schechner's project first the Warsaw boy is shown on screen. The camera zooms in on the right hand of the little boy, which has been
digitally manipulated in such a way that he seems to be holding a
photograph in that hand, the photograph of the Palestinian boy,
being hauled off by Israeli soldiers. He too holds an image in his
hand, that of the Jewish boy in the Warsaw Ghetto. Schechner
thus presents the two children as calling out to the viewer that
each of them protests against the suffering inflicted on the other,
creating a bond of empathy across time, across history.[15]

This most clearly highlights what I intend the metaphor of
nomadic images to mean. If Steichen saw fit to use individual
photographs irrespective of authorial intent, rearranging and recontextualizing them as he pleased, Schechner through digital
manipulation takes this process a few radical steps further. He
takes what he sees as free-ranging, roving images, instantly and
widely recognized, and does intrusive surgery on them. He thus
takes away whatever autonomy they had as individual images,
representing moments in history that had occurred before the
eye of a camera, in order to produce virtual realities. Nomadic
images never resist, never protest, even when put in the service of
eliciting protest and anger among the viewers. The manipulation
of images, which has occurred since the beginning of photography, has reached an unprecedented stage of manipulating the
viewers. Nomadic images are like so many Lego pieces that can
be endlessly put together to form ever new constructions—of
reality, of meaning.

But how about the authenticity and veracity of photographic

images? If artists should feel free to do with photographic images as they please, who should feel responsible for preserving
photographs in their status as historical documents? Raising the
question is answering it. It is for historians always to see it as
their assigned task and duty to retrace the trajectory of nomadic
images and take them back to the moment in time when what
these images show in fact happened before the camera's eye. Nor
should historians stop there. First on their agenda is to tell the
story not only of what happened, but why it happened and under
what precise circumstances. Thus they will add a resonance to
photographic images that, if anything, will only add to the accrued meanings of their nomadic afterlife. Secondly, they should
feel free to move on from there and not stop at the point where
the afterlife of images begins; after all, this is the point at which
histories open up of contested readings worthy of the art and
craft of historians. They should do this with their eyes open to
settings and contexts for reception and for the ironies of historical memory. If the subject is the remembrance of the Holocaust,
the obvious question to raise is how differently people live with
its memory in settings far removed from the countries and cultures where it took place. There is a strong and vivid memory
culture concerning the Holocaust in the United States, and historians have been engaged in trying to grasp what was behind the
ebbs and flows in America's memory of the Holocaust. Visual
sources have crucially informed this history, even if it is a matter,
paradoxically, of roving images that in the manner of true no-
mads know no bounds and have a history of circulating on both
sides of the Atlantic.

[8]

BARACK HUSSEIN OBAMA:
TWO PORTRAIT SKETCHES

Barack Hussein Obama: His Powers
of Language, His Language of Power

OF BILL CLINTON it has been said that he was America's first black president because of his apparent affinity with America's black population. Of Barack Obama it might be said that he is America's first "white president of color." From the first moment he entered public life, none of the templates that Americans use to handle the racial and ethnic diversity of their compatriots seemed to apply. Obama seemed equally at ease presenting himself as a person of white origin or as the son of an immigrant from Kenya. His life history and formative experiences allowed him to affiliate with black and white, with poor and rich, with the world of Christianity and Islam. He had spent part of his life growing up in those different worlds. A leading black intellectual in America, Harvard sociologist Orlando Patterson, recognized these qualities in the early days of Obama's rise as a political phenomenon: "Most whites don't feel threatened by him. Even moderate racists—not the hard core, obviously—can say 'I like this guy.' For the first time they feel at ease with a black man: he gives them the feeling that they are not racists."[1] Patterson himself, an immigrant from the Caribbean, like so many black immigrants feels difference from and distance toward America's native black population. Although perceived and treated as just another black person by America's white population, black immigrants elude such profiling. They are more socially mobile than the average American-born blacks and have more often reached positions of leadership—such as Marcus Garvey in the 1920s, Stokely Carmichael in the 1960s, or Colin Powell in the late twentieth century.

Obama resembles such immigrant blacks in the greater freedom of affiliation he may have felt was open to him. His time as a community developer on Chicago's South Side where he worked for poor whites and blacks helped him give sense and purpose to his life. Yet at the same time he moved in leading intellectual circles at the University of Chicago. His sense of affiliation with America's black population may be reflected in his choice of a marriage partner, Michelle Obama. Unlike her husband she stems from what Dutch historian Jan Willem Schulte Nordholt once called "the people that walk in darkness," the title to his history of America's black population.[2] It is a fitting image for a population group that in its collective memory of slavery, repression, and the struggle for emancipation and civil rights has indeed come to resemble a nation unto itself. But to the extent that this shared recollection of white racism, of exploitation and discrimination, still feeds a reservoir of hatred and anger among America's blacks, Obama forms no part of it. The test came when in the run-up to the presidential election, at the height of the campaign, Obama's trusted friend and confidant, black preacher Jeremiah Wright, raged against America's sustained racism, domestically and internationally. Obama felt forced to respond in an impressive public address in Philadelphia, reminding all Americans of the high ideals that from its inception had inspired the American republic.[3] At the same time Obama reminded Americans of the long history of compromise between these ideals and the practice of slavery. Obama used his oratorical mastery to call on Americans not to use their history as a source of division, inspiring the sort of "incendiary language to express views that have the potential not only to widen the racial divide, but views that denigrate both the greatness and the goodness of our nation; that rightly offend white and black alike." This, like many other of Obama's public addresses, is still accessible on the Internet. It is this use of the Internet as a medium of mass communication that is typical of Obama's political style. He has radically broken with the mindless reduction of political debate to the mere sound and fury of inane "sound bites." He takes his time to develop his thoughts, thus inviting his audience to take its time for reflecting on them.

An illustrious precursor like President Abraham Lincoln, past master in America's rhetorical tradition, had experienced the problem of slavery as posing the central dilemma in his political life. He famously found the rhetorical language to express this dilemma, as in his "House Divided" speech (a "house," that is to say the Union, the United States, will not stand if it is divided against itself, half slave, and half free). Lincoln, as a statesman who found himself caught on the horns of this dilemma, felt forced to find a compromise solution between two ideals, of emancipating the slave population and of preserving the Union. Tragically torn between the two, he reached the conclusion that preserving the Union, in order to save America's Great Experiment in democratic self-government, must weigh in more heavily than the emancipation of the slaves. As he put it: "If I could save the Union without freeing *any* slave I would do it, and if I could save it by freeing *all* the slaves I would do it; and if I could save it by freeing some and leaving others alone I would also do that."[4] Addressing his democratic audience Lincoln offered no easy answers. Rather than use the power of public speech to delude his audience with rousing visions of a beckoning future, he invited it to ponder the complexities of the present. While evoking the inspirational history of American ideals, in the grand manner of the American Jeremiad, as Sacvan Bercovitch called it, he publicly shared his inner torment in the face of the ethical dilemmas that confronted him.[5]

Like Lincoln, Obama has proved a master of public speech.

In his relatively short public career, he has used the power of rhetoric to bring messages of hope and new beginnings, inspiring people to follow and support him. But like Lincoln, he also used his rhetorical mastery, during the campaign as well as in his presidency, publicly to account for the dilemmas he confronted and the conscientious choices he saw had to be made. Yet, in politics, as Lincoln was well aware, rhetorical visions in the end always have to face the test of reality, of practical action. Rhetoric at some point must translate into action if it is not to lose its power of persuasion. This clear and present danger became manifest shortly after Obama's accession to the presidency. Soon it appeared that the enthusiasm he had inspired among his followers turned into disillusionment, a sense that he was no more than a "faux liberal." At the time of his Cairo speech, in June 2009, before a student audience but addressed at the larger world of Islam, this was the general response among the audience: the words were fine, but where were the actions?[6] When Obama first entered the fray of the Israeli-Palestinian conflict, demanding radical change in the way Israel behaved in the occupied Palestinian territories, the general impression prevailed that Israel had quickly called Obama's bluff. Ever since, Obama has appeared unable to face up to the entrenched lobbies and veto groups, at home or abroad, preventing even minimal progress toward a future so eloquently evoked in speech. More generally, when held up against the daring visions outlined in speech after speech, in areas of foreign or domestic policy, Obama's actions were deemed wanting. Rather than riding the groundswell of support that carried him into the White House, he has seemed to be leading from behind, leaving it to entrenched power balances in Washington politics or in the international arena to work out compromise solutions for him to endorse. Too rarely, it seemed, did he choose to rise above the din of partisan votes and voices to speak in his own voice, addressing the nation to rekindle the enthusiasms among the larger populace that had carried him into the White House. Too often did he seem to leave the field where public opinion plays itself out to the demolition crews spurred on by right-wing media and an obstructionist opposition, in Congress and in the country.

There is an enigmatic side to Obama in all this. While patiently riding out storms, he has managed to build a solid record of legislative achievement. If patience is one of Obama's strengths, he nonetheless may have neglected to exert his talents in setting the terms of public debate, in constructing a winning narrative to present and explain his achievements. Patience is a quality direly lacking among the larger population, whose mood is set by frenzy and urgency better served, it seems, by sloganeering Tea Party populists, promising to "take America back." This rampant anti-intellectualism leaves little room for Obama to keep his Olympian cool. Spurred into rhetorical action by the 2010 midterm elections, his rather lame contribution to public discourse was his call that having worked hard to change the guard, now was the time to guard the change.[7] It didn't do much to change the terms of public debate.

Yet when the occasion presents itself, Obama can rise to it and eloquently address the dilemmas of power as he perceives them. An impressive example is his speech in Oslo on his acceptance of the Nobel Peace Prize. The Oslo Nobel Committee's decision had met with widespread cynical glee. Here was a man receiving a peace prize who shortly before had decided in favor of a military surge in Afghanistan. Obama did not share in the cynicism when accepting the prize. In a characteristic, conscientious speech he accounted for the path he had chosen to follow between the goal of peace and understanding in the world and the rival goal of national security in a world where good and evil are locked in combat. There were those who heard echoes of George W. Bush, who had turned "evil" into a facile sound bite and used it as a sufficient explanation of what moves the terrorists of this world. Obama, on the other hand, invites further reflection and intellectual struggle with the problem of evil. One may of course beg to differ and not quite see Obama's strategic decisions as serving

America's security interests in the long run. Yet, simply looking at the time for deliberation Obama had taken for reaching his decision, weighing a great number of policy options against each other, shows that he is a different political animal than his predecessor, in the latter's unseemly rush to invade Iraq. It would be hard to see Obama as a pliable puppet in the hands of entrenched power groups in Washington.

At the top of his rhetorical mastery, in speeches concerning racism as a divisive force in American society, or the use of military power in foreign policy, Obama finds his place in America's great tradition of the statesman as public orator and master of rhetoric. In that role he explains, renders account, and invites the public to reflect. Obama is keenly aware of this long line of history, using it to place himself squarely in an American political tradition.[8] Repeatedly he takes his cue from inspiring predecessors. Taking this inspirational role Obama not only addresses his fellow Americans, inciting them to political participation. He also speaks to the world, rekindling an enthusiasm for American leadership after the damage done to it during eight long years of the Bush presidency. When still a candidate vying for the presidency, Obama gave a speech in Berlin, on July 24, 2008, before a crowd of thousands whose lost hopes for the United States Obama seemed to restore and personify.[9] In fine rhetorical balance he brought together a reference to the Berlin Wall with Lincoln's metaphor of the house divided. It brought the audience in mind of Kennedy's famous "Ich bin ein Berliner" speech, delivered during his visit to Berlin in the days of the Cold War. Obama wanted to present himself as the embodiment of an America with which Europeans could once again feel affiliated: "The walls between old allies on either side of the Atlantic cannot stand." Thus in a city not long before divided by a wall—"divided against itself"—Lincoln's words assumed a poignant resonance, and called forth an association with his "half slave, half free." When words like these come from the mouths of Americans, the danger is always of an implied missionary zeal, of interventionist intentions even, particularly today after the cynical misuse of similar language to justify military adventurism by the Bush administration. Obama is too much like Lincoln in his awareness of the tragic tension between politics and ethics, between idealism and realism. When confronting such hard choices he is rather a man of steel, not the weed that waves with the tides. He does not hesitate to speak his mind on matters of great concern to him, whether it is bankers and their obscene remunerations, or the failing security apparatus in America. The Homeland Security bureaucracy was in for a hiding, when Obama publicly argued that it is incapable of connecting the dots on a map of imminent threats and simply reproduces the intelligence failures of pre-9/11 days. Bush has never been willing to own up to such failures. His response was simply to pile on new bureaucratic layers, compounding the problem.[10]

Even his most fervent supporters must have felt for Obama when he acceded to the presidency in view of the shambles, domestically and internationally, that the Bush administration had left in its wake. The discomfiture of an economic system, wars without end, the continuing threat of terrorism, an unprecedented level of partisan division, were the dish that was set before the new president. No way could he hope to start with a clean slate. Probably the greatest paradox that Obama had to face up to was the deeply ingrained antistatism among Americans. According to opinion polls majorities among them wish for better health care, better education, better infrastructure, yet are opposed to concerted government efforts to tackle such problems, rallying against them with hysterical cries of "socialism." This intuitive distrust had received official blessing since the Reagan years and its view of government as "not the solution, but part of the problem." But the paradox goes back further in time and can be discerned from the early opposition to Roosevelt's New Deal project. Ever since, the pattern of support for and opposition to a view of government as the collective instrument for pursuing the public interest has hardened into the partisan mold of Democrats versus Republicans. The New Deal, supported by a coalition of forces known as the Roosevelt coalition, constituting the Democratic Party that for decades assumed the role of the natural party of government, gave rise to the slow and contested early formation of a welfare state on American soil. Incrementally, step by step, its further development took place under Democratic Party auspices well into the 1960s. Obama wishes to continue in that tradition, albeit in a political climate more resistant than ever before. The solid Democratic Party majority in both houses of Congress since the 2008 elections may have seemed to open a window of opportunity, yet the hardening of political support and opposition, if not obstruction, along strictly partisan lines, in addition to the loud-mouthed populism in the media and among the population at large, never boded well.

In view of the forbidding pile of problems that Obama has had to confront, it was clear that he needed time. Yet time has been running out fast. If Obama manages to ride out the storm of populist and right-wing obstruction, he may in the end effect a change in the political climate, if not the political culture of the country, not unlike the late 1930s. Then, the continuing Depression had offered Roosevelt the opportunity to bring about a culture that gave central place to a sense of solidarity and collective endeavor. The period might be referred to as a populist moment in American history, in the sense that Lawrence Goodwyn used those words for an earlier period in American history, describing functioning political institutions constructed in terms of an inclusive populist paradigm but only for a historical "moment."[11] The late 1930s and early 1940s may have been another such moment of inclusiveness, centering on "the people" and "the common man" not only as rhetorical figures of speech but also as central subjects of collective action, brought together around government as the collective body in charge of seeing to the common interest, the "res publica." In this role government had not only sponsored many employment programs but also, for the first time in American history, had seen fit to sponsor the arts. Thus it promoted a range of artistic projects that aimed at the common people as its audience. In literature, in music and the theater, in photography and painting, artists went through a vernacular, or folk, period in their careers. They chose to descend from their elitist, ivory towers and opened themselves up to the common American as their public, which, in government-sponsored projects, they set out to serve.

A prime example of this trend is the work of American composer Aaron Copland. Orienting himself in the 1920s upon the international musical avant-garde, in the late 1930s he turned to the use of American folk repertoire to find his vernacular voice. A typical composition in this vein is his *Fanfare for the Common Man*, an ode to the common man seen as the central support of American democracy. Another composition from this period—the *Lincoln Portrait* of 1944—is an ode to Lincoln, or rather to his inspired use of language. At precisely the time that Roosevelt himself powerfully availed himself of America's hallowed rhetorical tradition, Copland reconnected to Lincoln's inspirational language. At the dramatic culmination of the piece Lincoln's urgent call, in the concluding words to his *Gettysburg Address*, words spoken on a Civil War battlefield, soar above the music: "that we here solemnly resolve that the dead shall not have died in vain, that this nation, under God, shall have a new birth of freedom; and that government of the people, by the people, and for the people shall not perish from the earth." There is a memorable television recording of a performance of the *Lincoln Portrait*, with the composer reciting and his former student Leonard Bernstein conducting. Visually Copland was no Lincoln. He was a shy and slightly awkward man, not the type expected of a public orator. Yet he managed to rise above himself when in his thin voice he took the text to its climax. In his modest way he brought an ode to Lincoln, or rather an ode to the high ideals of democracy.

There are many enlightening studies, by Garry Wills among others, of Lincoln's use of public speech, of his rhetorical mastery.[12]

But rarely does this mastery affect us as strongly as in Copland's musical tribute. Something like that same mastery we may recognize in Obama's political appeal. It already is his solid claim to fame. At the time of this writing he has been in power for more than two years and has a solid record of legislative achievement. It is to be hoped that he has many more years to translate his inspired and inspirational visions in speech as well as in action. Perhaps he will prove able to revive the broad alliance of enthused voters that, like a virtual Internet community, carried him to the presidency and to turn it into a lasting support of his political power. To that end he must remain what he had been for so many during the campaign, a man holding high the hopes of a new beginning. Tied up as he is now in the imbroglio of Washington politics, he must at the same time, much like Roosevelt, rise above it and reach out to his nationwide constituency. He must keep alive a sense of closeness and inclusion among his supporters, rather than leave them mired in alienation. If successful, Obama may well lead Americans on the way to overcoming their internal divisions and once again inspire, as under Roosevelt, a sense of common effort and collective destiny. And who knows, a new Copland may arise to give musical expression to such a new political and cultural climate.

Barack Hussein Obama: American President

Barack Hussein Obama: American president. Do we need to make the point when the Obama administration is well on the way to the next presidential election? For sizable segments of the electorate the answer would have to be "yes." According to a CNN/Opinion Research Corporation survey, more than a quarter of the public have doubts about Obama's citizenship, with 11 percent saying that Obama was definitely not born in the United States and another 16 percent saying that the president was probably not born in the country.[13] These doubters are called birthers. Their numbers are swelled by those who call Obama fascist or communist, anything to make him and his policies sound anti-American, or un-American. They all speak in the voice of a white nationalism that lives by the myth of a "real America," as evoked by Sarah Palin on the campaign trail.[14] Ironically, at the same time, a debate was going on among America's black population over whether Obama, given his biography, could ever affiliate with the sense of history and identity of blacks born and raised in the United States. "Black nativism" was what Orlando Patterson, himself an immigrant from the Caribbean rather than a native-born black, called this exclusionary attitude.[15]

From his early days as a public figure Obama made it a point of placing himself squarely in an American intellectual and political tradition as he chose to define it. In his writings, particularly his two published books, as well as in his public addresses, beginning with his memorable keynote address at the Democratic Convention in 2004, he evokes an inspirational America, whose past should serve as a guide to its future.[16] In the speech Obama weaves his own story into that of the American republic, presenting himself as emblematic of a larger American promise fulfilled. In his meteoric rise to the presidency, Obama has been his own best advocate. Yet now, caught in the thicket of politics, it seems on occasion as if he can use all the help he can get in affirming the Americanness of his ideas and his political action. Many of his early enthusiastic supporters have turned away in disgust at what they see as a political practice of compromise and sell-out; many on the right have found their voice in Tea Party calls for "taking America back."

Among the more Olympian voices to be heard in Obama's defense is that of James T. Kloppenberg. He is the most prominent among those who set out to establish connections between their "reading" of Obama and their reading of America's intellectual and political history.[17] One crucial connection is with arguably the most American style of philosophy: pragmatism. It inspired Obama's perspective on America's constitutional history as one continuing intellectual debate, centered on commonly held values, in what he calls a "deliberative democracy." Whereas many activists on both the left and the right proclaim their incommensurable principles with the fervor of true believers, Obama sees things differently. In his speech marking the end of U.S. military engagement in Iraq, on August 31, 2010, Obama declared, "The greatness of our democracy is grounded in our ability to move beyond our differences, and to learn from our experience as we confront the many challenges ahead." As Kloppenberg points out: "That single sentence encapsulates Obama's commitments to deliberative democracy and pragmatism, the signature features of the approach to American history and politics he adopts in his writings and his speeches."[18]

Reading Kloppenberg put me in mind of an earlier episode in the writing of political history-in-the-making. President Obama is not the first president who sees himself confronted with suspicions concerning the Americanness of his motives and actions. Before him, President Franklin D. Roosevelt had similar aspersions to contend with. In the post–World War II years historians of a Democratic bent took it upon themselves to defend the Roosevelt heritage by arguing the basic Americanness of the Roosevelt approach to politics. There were many occasions for this moment in American historiography, commonly known as the Consensus School. Domestically, there was the pent-up resentment of the Republican Party, out to roll back as many of the gains as possible achieved under Roosevelt, gains benefiting organized labor, gains giving rise to social security and welfare state provisions, gains finally in setting up the state itself as an agent for the Common Weal. How very un-American indeed. Internationally, there was the Cold War, a confrontation with a closed ideological system—communism—following on the heels of the war against fascism and National Socialism. If Roosevelt, throughout his years in office, had always had to confront the dilemma of not being sufficiently to the left in the eyes of his left-wing supporters, or way too much on the left in the eyes of conservatives, the consensus historians chose to see Roosevelt as typically the pragmatist, averse from ideological closure and doctrinaire thinking. He was presented as inhabiting what Arthur M. Schlesinger, Jr., called "the vital center," the pragmatic place halfway between the two opposed ideological extremes. Other consensus historians, such as Daniel Boorstin, Richard Hofstadter, Louis Hartz, in their evocation of an American liberal tradition and a liberal consensus, saw ideology—as Boorstin had it in his analysis of the genius of American politics—as never more than a self-evident "given." According to this collective apologia for Roosevelt's political practice, it had stood squarely within an American political tradition, seen as nonideological, pragmatic, and deliberative.[19] The consensus historians have done for Roosevelt what Kloppenberg and others are now doing in behalf of Obama.

Yet there are more ways in which to cast Obama's policies and actions as typical of an American president. Kloppenberg's way is the high-minded road to establishing Obama's presidency as rooted in American traditions, focusing on the American ideas and ideals that have inspired Obama as a political man. Another way would be to look at Obama as a political actor and to ask ourselves whether his leadership in the thicket of politics is representative of a longer history of American political practice.

[9]

OBAMA AND THE PARADOX OF AMERICAN
GLOBAL POWER: DREAMS OF DEMOCRACY
AND THE IMPERIAL IMPERATIVE

AMERICA'S POWER AND presence in the world are still unrivaled.
One connection between its power and presence is through a
worldwide system of military bases, whose number is about
a thousand. It is a system of high interconnectivity, involving
cutting-edge communications technology. Pinpoint military actions take place by remote control from halfway around the
globe by people sitting at consoles at nodal points in the communication web. This configuration of power and military hard-
ware conjures up an image of empire of worldwide reach. As
such the United States faces the central concern of every empire
before it: the control of sources of unrest and restiveness within
the limits of its imperial reach. In other words, it is subject to
what we might call the imperial imperative. Empire is as empire
does.

How does this square with the long-established view, among
Americans as well as among those peoples at the receiving end
of America's imperial sway, of America as a benevolent power,
a guardian of democracy and political freedoms? What, if anything, has changed in America's international presence? Is it a
matter of perception only, of people waking up to the reality

of the exercise of power, or have America's foreign policy elites fallen prey to the dictates of imperial leadership?

This essay will address these two questions. Can the United States be meaningfully seen as an empire in the ways it has behaved since entering the world stage as a central player after World War II? Secondly, if it is an empire, how has this affected the quality of its democratic life and institutions? One central hypothesis connects both explorations. It can be formulated as follows: if there is a logic to the life of empires that one might call the imperial imperative—a logic according to which the pursuit of hegemonic control to the far periphery of empire calls for ever greater concentration of power at the center—the United States too will show the effects of this logic. In spite of its creed of democracy and republicanism the U.S., acting as an empire, cannot escape this imperial imperative. An obvious test case is offered by the two recent presidencies of George W. Bush and of Barack Hussein Obama. Although the latter presented himself as the anti-Bush, opposing all transgressions of constitutional constraints that his predecessor had stood for, and promising to take America back to its first republican principles, the imperial imperative, according to our hypothesis, would prevent Obama from pursuing such a course.

Democracy and the Imperial Imperative

On December 6, 2011, President Obama followed in President Theodore Roosevelt's footsteps and delivered a speech in Osawatomie, Kansas. "In 1910," as he reminded his audience, "Teddy Roosevelt came here to Osawatomie and he laid out his vision for what he called a New Nationalism. 'Our country,' he said, 'means nothing unless it means the triumph of a real democracy . . . of an economic system under which each man shall be guaranteed the opportunity to show the best that there is in him.'" Like Roosevelt before him, Obama had come wielding a big stick, holding forth against political gridlock in Washington politics, and the ideological stranglehold of the "You're on your own" economics of Republicans. The "raging debate over the best way to restore growth and prosperity, restore balance, restore fairness," Obama argued, is "the defining issue of our time." Obama pointed to the growing inequality and income disparity in American society: "Inequality also distorts our democracy. It gives an outsized voice to the few who can afford high-priced lobbyists and unlimited campaign contributions, and it runs the risk of selling out our democracy to the highest bidder. It leaves everyone else rightly suspicious that the system in Washington is rigged against them, that our elected representatives aren't looking out for the interests of most Americans." Like Roosevelt before him, Obama spoke on behalf of a more inclusive view of democracy and the national interest.

On another Rooseveltian theme, though, the theme of empire and the way it affects democracy, Obama was strangely silent. And not only in Osawatomie. It is a theme that had divided Rooseveltian Progressives against themselves, with minority voices like that of Jane Addams warning of imperialism's baneful impact on democracy at home. It is a theme that on similar grounds Obama might have seen as equally a defining issue of our time.

At the top of his rhetorical mastery, in speeches concerning racism as a divisive force in American society, or the use of military power in foreign policy, Obama finds his place in America's great tradition of the statesman as public orator and master of rhetoric. In that role he explains, renders account, and invites the public to reflect. Obama is keenly aware of this long line of history, using it to place himself squarely in an American political tradition. When acceding to the presidency in early 2009, Barack Obama appeared as the anti-Bush that many during the campaign had come to see in him. When he took the oath of office, swearing to defend and uphold the Constitution of the United States, it seemed like the first step in rolling back the relentless encroachment upon the restraints of executive power set by the Constitution and by international law as endorsed by the United States. Obama had all the right credentials for this role. As a senator he had voted against the war in Iraq as an illegal war of aggression. As a candidate he promised to close Guantanamo Bay's detention center, which in the eyes of the world had come to symbolize the illegitimacy of the ways in which the United States, under President Bush, had chosen to wage its global war on terrorism. Obama appeared like the man who would bring to light the dark and secret world, beyond the reach of law and legal protections, that America had ventured upon, a world of illegal surveillance of its own citizenry, a world of secret renditions of terrorist suspects, and of torture and high-tech retaliatory assassination. He appeared to bring a promise of ending all this and returning to a presidency under the law, rather than above it. In words from his inaugural address: "My administration is committed to creating an unprecedented level of openness in government."

If hopes were pinned so high on the Obama presidency, how would this square with the trends in American presidential leadership that come under such names as the unitary executive, or the imperial presidency? The trend was seen by many observers, in the United States and Europe, as a continued erosion of America's democratic and constitutional order, a continued power grab by the American president who as chief executive officer in charge of the national interest felt unduly hampered by established constitutional constraints, such as the institutional checks and balances or the constitutional protection of civil rights and civil liberties. Ever more intrusive in the fabric of social relations in the name of antiterrorist surveillance, ever more scornful of institutional countervailing powers, the Bush presidency subverted the American constitution, although held by oath to protect it. This can be seen as only the latest, most daring, version of what Arthur Schlesinger in his 1968 book *The Imperial Presidency* had held out as a warning to Americans.[1]

In fact this suspicion of slow democratic erosion goes back further, to such World War I American pacifists as Jane Addams, who reminded Americans of the connection between a warfare state and dictatorship. Precisely Bush's war on terrorism, a war without an exit option, allowed him to venture ever further on the way to the unitary executive. Thus he rewrote legislation, duly enacted by Congress, with signing statements giving him leeway not to implement laws as enacted. Thus he could create dark zones beyond the reach of American law, such as most ignominiously at Guantanamo Bay. Glaring examples abound. When President Bush signed a new law, sponsored by Senator McCain, restricting the use of torture when interrogating detainees, he also issued a presidential signing statement. That statement asserted that his power as commander-in-chief gave him the authority to bypass the very law he had just signed. This news came fast on the heels of Bush's admission that, since 2002, he had repeatedly authorized the National Security Agency to conduct electronic surveillance without a warrant, in flagrant violation of applicable federal law. And before that, Bush had declared he had the unilateral authority to ignore the Geneva Conventions and indefinitely to detain without due process both immigrants and citizens as enemy combatants. The pattern behind all these blatant presidential encroachments on the law and the Constitution led to pointed revisits, in the later years of the Bush administration, of the phrase "unitary executive" as almost a code word for a doctrine favoring unfettered executive power.[2]

Many of the worries and concerns in Europe about this imperial drift in American politics fed directly into Europe's feelings of anti-Americanism. Hopes were that Obama, taking his oratorical cues from Lincoln, Roosevelt, Kennedy, and Martin Luther King, might indeed take the United States back to its first high principles (which, as Machiavelli reminds us, is the central recipe for preserving a republic). This would require a more direct, and intellectually articulate, communication with his American and world audience. Yet, given the pressure on him to exert his leadership as a president who called the war in Afghanistan a "war of necessity," temptations were great to cut constitutional corners in the manner of his predecessor. Obama may find it hard to give up gains in executive power as they have accrued to the presidency over the preceding years. Yet in a democratic spirit, upholding the Constitution, while scaling back some of the legal enormities of the Bush administration, he must be held to develop ways of forceful leadership that Americans and non-Americans alike will see as convincing and legitimate.

At present, though, things do not bode well. In fact, many signs point rather in the direction of continuity with Bush administration practices. Thus, in the crucial civil rights area of the treatment of detainees held in the context of the war on terror, the Obama administration took steps and invented arguments to maintain the power to imprison terrorism suspects for extended periods without judicial oversight—most recently, in 2012, in the National Defense Authorization Act. The man who as presidential candidate had still spoken of the false choice between fighting terrorism and respecting habeas corpus, and who had rejected the Bush administration's attempt at creating a black hole at Guantanamo, now did exactly that by moving detainees to Bagram airbase, beyond the reach of constitutional protections.[3] In the same vein, the man who, as presidential candidate reminded his audience that as a former constitutional law professor he would, unlike the current president (that is, George W. Bush), actually respect the Constitution, acted in contravention of the 1973 War Powers Resolution adopted by Congress when he authorized U.S. military intervention in Libya.[4] In the tortured language of Orwellian newspeak, Obama denied the Libyan intervention was a war at all. Hence, the War Powers Resolution did not apply.[5] Ironically, Obama thus cast aside a congressional resolution whose intention it had been to restore the balance between the powers of Congress and the presidency after years of the balance tilting toward the executive.

As a further point, rather than the government itself living up to its promise of "unprecedented openness," we see a resurgence of leakers of secret government policies—of "whistleblowers," most famously including Julian Assange, Bradley (now Chelsea) Manning, and Edward Snowden—reminiscent of the days of the leaked Pentagon Papers. The culmination points so far have been the flood of Wikileaks foreign policy documents, followed by the massive leaks of documents concerning the work of the NSA. The Obama administration's response was vindictive and very much in the manner of an insulted sovereign. In the manner of a unitary executive, without due process, it held an alleged leaker of documents, Bradley Manning, in solitary confinement, and stepped into the field of economic transactions, blocking credit card payments to Wikileaks, in addition to pressuring foreign governments in its search for the main culprit, Julian Assange.[6] The administration would have acted similarly in the case of Edward Snowden, had he not found sanctuary in, of all places, Russia. Even before the Wikileaks furor, though, the *New York Review of Books,* over the names of left-wing luminaries including Daniel Ellsberg of Pentagon Papers fame, published a paid, page-long call "To end the complicity of silence," reminding the readers that "Crimes are Crimes No Matter Who Does Them." Side by side are two portraits of Bush Jr. and Obama linked by this caption: "Crimes under Bush are crimes under Obama and must be resisted by anyone who claims a shred of conscience."[7] High on the list of government abominations is the freedom it takes in composing lists of suspects of terrorism, including U.S. citizens, selected for assassination. The text goes on to indict the Obama administration for expanding the use of drone attacks and for arguing that the United States has the authority under international law to use extrajudicial killing in sovereign countries with which it is not at war. Such acts have now been consecrated into "standard operating procedure" by Obama, who claims, as did Bush, executive privilege and state secrecy in times of war as he defines it. Like Bush, Obama uses pliant legal counselors where he can find them, in the White House, the Pentagon, the

State Department, or the Department of Justice—that is, from within the executive bureaucracy—to produce legal memoranda waiving legal restraints on the executive in the defense of the national interest.

Like the phrase "unitary executive," the words "executive privilege" are suggestive of constitutional law doctrines justifying the leeway presidents grant themselves in their unilateral choice of means in defense of the national interest. On previous occasions, as in the Truman Steel Seizure Case or the Nixon administration's refusal to make public the Oval Office secret tapes, the claim of executive privilege was tested by the Supreme Court and found wanting.[8] The Obama administration has not yet come up to a similar test. Not surprisingly, the president has seen his policies of secrecy given the blessing of conservative commentators. In an op-ed piece in the *Wall Street Journal*, entitled "Barack Obama: Defender of State Secrets," Gabriel Schoenfeld, a senior fellow at the Hudson Institute, had this to say: "It is not an overstatement to say that secrecy today is one of the most critical tools of national defense. Leaks of counterterrorism secrets to the press, and disclosure of counterterrorism techniques and procedures in courtrooms, can imperil the war effort. We are thus faced squarely with the abiding tension between liberty and security." What Schoenfeld calls the "carping civil-libertarian critics" may, as he admits, serve a useful purpose in guarding against government excesses. But Schoenfeld goes on to conclude that "the more voluble they become, the more apparent it also becomes that Mr. Obama is doing the right thing."[9] Judged by the company Obama attracts, we would be hard put to recognize in him what so many during the campaign had hopefully anticipated. As president he found himself in a role as commander-in-chief, fighting two ground wars and a more general one against the elusive enemy of global terrorism, without a clear exit strategy. They are wars he took over when entering office, and that he has pursued by means that make it hard to see a personal touch to distinguish him from his predecessor, let alone to recognize the signs of a transformational presidency. Yet those were the words that Colin Powell, a black Republican, used in his quiet and eloquent television endorsement of Obama during the electoral campaign.[10] There is irony today in referring back to this moment. Here we had a man who had given his name to a military doctrine, the Powell doctrine, reminding military planners never to enter a war without a clear exit strategy. Yet well into his presidency President Obama was mired in wars without exit strategies, expanding programs of secret action in the Middle East, without any prospect of the endeavor holding the promise of a new beginning.[11] But more than that, Obama seems mired in the insider ways of Washington while losing the rapport he had with the broad constituency that carried him to the presidency. If his march to the White House testified to the power of rhetoric, Obama has found no way yet, it seems, to use the presidency as a bully pulpit to engage and educate his public in the moral dilemmas of the exercise of power. In other words, he has not yet developed a rhetoric of power.

Such a demanding form of rhetorical discourse would, of course, call for more than Bush's sound bite uttered with a smirk: "I am the decider,"[12] or more generally the boastful language accompanying America's position as "sole remaining superpower" following the collapse of the Soviet Union. If there was a rhetoric of power discernible at all in those days, it was the language of arms speaking, of a Wilsonianism in boots, or of the "shock and awe" inspired by America's arsenal of high-tech weapons. In contrast to this, a rhetoric of power, as I here envision it, would demand Obama once again to rise above himself, above the din of voices in Washington circles and the media, and to address the ethical dilemmas and quandaries of democratic leadership, to address the tension between secrecy and national security, and to become the democratic educator that Lincoln was before him. It would entail more than the rhetorical projection of power in the face of external threats confronting the nation, more than the construction of an enemy image and the demonization of the enemy, as in president Reagan's rhetoric of power, when he spoke of the Soviet Union as "the evil empire."[13] It would entail rendering a public account of the unintended consequences of the uses of power, as they range from open military confrontation, and its accompanying "collateral damage" of civilians killed by U.S. fire, to secret programs of assassination, rendition, and imprisonment. These are all means of confrontation that may well result in swelling the ranks of enemy forces rather than quelling them. Using public speech to convey such a sense of irony, if not of the tragic quality of democratic leadership, is a tall order and does not necessarily go down well with the larger public. When President Carter tried to wean Americans off the conventional rhetoric of the Cold War, speaking instead of the "inordinate fear of Communism,"[14] it was taken as a sign of softness, if not weakness.

The problem confronting President Obama in this respect is that on a number of occasions he has, in public speeches, reached out toward the Muslim world, trying to take away its inordinate fear of the United States, and to contribute to mutual understanding through diplomatic means and the power of public speech. Yet, neither in the Middle East nor among the American public, has he managed to reconcile his guiding visions with the actual policies that he pursues or has left in place.

Addressing the Chicago Council of Global Affairs on April 23, 2007, when still a Democratic senator and presidential hopeful, Barack Obama said: "I still believe that America is the last, best hope of Earth. We just have to show the world why this is so. This President (that is, George W. Bush) may occupy the White House, but for the last six years the position of leader of the free world has remained open. And it's time to fill that role once more. The American moment has not passed. The American moment is here. And like generations before us, we will seize that moment, and begin the world anew."[15] Casting himself as a Promethean pretender to the role of leader of the free world, he could never hope to make a fresh start with a clean slate.

While aiming at beginning the world anew, he had to confront a world as it was left to him, like a chess player taking over a game halfway through, confronting all the constraints set before him. Entering the Washington corridors of power, with a freshly won mandate, must have felt like stepping into an arena ring-fenced by entrenched interests, veto groups, and contending ideological views of the national interest and America's place as a world power.

In 2011 it was fifty years since President Eisenhower had left office and had used the occasion to reflect on the ominous rise of what he called the military-industrial complex, commonly referred to later as the military-industrial-political complex. Eisenhower, at the height of the Cold War, warned against an American foreign policy set on a course of undue militarization, while undermining America's democratic ways.[16] Ironically, it was only after the Cold War and the collapse of the Soviet Union that such militarization proceeded apace. What had been gestating as a neoconservative project, envisioning a twenty-first-century America whose military power would be unrivaled and preeminent, now became the accepted discourse, touted by right-wing politicians and media pundits alike.

Currently, the American defense budget approaches the combined defense budgets of all other nations, friends and foes combined. U.S. defense outlays now consume roughly half of all federal discretionary dollars. The United States now has between seven hundred and a thousand military bases all over the globe, with new construction of drone bases proceeding apace. It can project military power in ever new technological ways. Yet if this policy is to be more than a very expensive insurance policy, against what threat, what enemy, is it meant to offer protection?

Here, I would argue, President Obama has his work cut out for him. Rather than letting himself be co-opted into this militarized view of the world and American foreign policy, it is not yet too late for him to grasp the moment and start to educate the American people. At a time when deficits at all levels of government threaten America's infrastructure, its education, health and welfare institutions, as well as its overall prosperity, Obama should address these issues by publicly reflecting on the costs of the current national security state, its financial costs as well as its human and political costs. As one opinion poll after another makes clear, the American people are stunningly unaware of such things. Given the right-wing control over the terms of public discourse, here is a challenge for the master of rhetoric that Obama has proven to be. Were he to take it up, it would be a new beginning indeed.

And yet, for a man with Obama's powers of speech there are strange moments of silence, of speechlessness. Surely, as on the occasion of the January 2011 point-blank fusillade in Tucson, where a deranged youngster wounded a congresswoman among a number of others and killed six people, among whom a young girl, Obama finds the words of consolation for grieving parents and a grieving nation. Rising above the toxic cesspool of what ranks as public debate and discourse in the United States today, he grasps the moment to educate the nation in the ways of civility and civilized debate. Yet when the child killed is not American, but a Pakistani or Afghan victim of the American way of war, killed on Obama's watch as commander-in-chief, he has not so far addressed the terrible moral dilemma that presents itself. Nor, more generally, does he speak to the central civil rights and human rights problems that his "targeted assassination" approach has opened up. Distant wars are being fought at the far-away *limes* of empire, passed over in silence, it may seem, by the American people. Yet, slowly but surely, the voice of a concerned public conscience is beginning to be heard, in the Blogosphere, and on the printed pages of America's leading intellectual journals and newspapers.

On only a few occasions so far has the Obama administration taken up the challenge and come up with a public account of its policy of targeted assassinations. On March 5, 2012, Attorney General Eric Holder, in a speech at Northwestern University's

Law School, essentially made the point that the United States is a
nation at war, facing "a nimble and determined enemy that cannot be underestimated."[17] Given such conditions of war, Holder
continued, "we must also recognize that there are instances
where our government has the clear authority . . . to defend the
United States through the appropriate and lawful use of lethal
force." By government Holder means the president, as the one
person to decide what is appropriate and lawful, the one person
who weighs the legalities of a case against the threat of imminent
danger. Under such conditions considerations of due process are
safe in the hands of the executive as sole protector of the national
security. It may not be due process as commonly understood, yet
people should rest assured that the president acts on mature consideration, following judicious process rather than formal due
process. Under conditions of war, the populace should take the
president's word for it that justice has been done. National defense has thus become a matter of presidential say-so. If Holder's
argument points in any clear direction, it is toward a continuing
"unitary executive," relentlessly eroding a government of law,
and under the law, as the United States has known and enjoyed
it for most of its history as a republic.[18]

A State of Exception?

Comparing the Bush Jr. and Obama presidencies, looking for
contrasts yet disturbingly finding continuities may leave one
clueless as to possible explanations. After all, when Obama first
acceded to the presidency, he had drawn clear lines to distinguish his administration from the preceding one. He would close
the Guantanamo Bay detention facility; he would end the use of
what euphemistically had become known as "enhanced interro-
gation techniques," or, more realistically, torture; he would end
the practice of so-called extraordinary rendition and the use of a
secret international network of "black holes" where terror suspects disappeared into extralegal limbo. In short he would end

all those transgressions of the ways of constitutional government that had stained America's image in the world and stoked the fires of anti-Americanism. He promised to take government back to transparency, the rule of law, and the protections of citizenship rights as guaranteed by the U.S. Constitution. Yet he refused to hold members of the previous administration to account, preferring to "look forward rather than backwards," as he put it. He preferred this to having it formally established in court when and where the previous administration had engaged in criminal behavior, breaking national and international law. In fact, his administration has fought the courts to block *civil* suits against torture perpetrators, claiming the privilege of state secrets.

This may have been dictated by political expedience. But was it also a political calculus when Obama early on called the war in Afghanistan a war of necessity, opting for an Iraq-like military surge before setting a deadline for the withdrawal of troops? Was it to protect his right flank, and fend off accusations of being soft on terrorism, when he stepped up the use of drones in the airspace of countries, such as Pakistan, with which the United States was not formally at war, or when he engaged in drawing up lists of people, U.S. citizens among them, to be killed without any form of due process or judicial oversight? Or do we need to look for another explanation when we wish to account for a disturbing range of counterterrorism policies that are ever more secretive, without check or balance, ever more intrusive into the privacy of individual citizens or the sovereignty of independent states, and yes, in disturbing continuity with many of the policies of the preceding administration in its war against terrorism?

One way to account for the continuity would be to see both administrations in the context of post-9/11 history, both equally involved in a continuing confrontation with terrorism as a global threat. Both administrations used the war against terrorism as justifying their transgressions of peace-time legal constraints. Secret memos produced by legal counsel from within the executive, such as the "torture memos" of the Bush years, or the memos justifying assassinations by drone in the first Obama administration, testify to this trend. In other words, they both claimed a state of exception to account for the way they curtailed citizens' freedoms and rights. Both administrations, one might argue, thus acted as all governments do when engaged in war. Wartime constraints, then, may be seen as exerting a stronger pull than any high-minded promises of a return to the rule of law. If so, Obama's policies may be seen as the hard-won lessons of realism forced upon a man of different inclinations.

But is this account really convincing? In spite of what in-house lawyers in the Bush and Obama administrations have argued, if the United States is really engaged in war, what sort of war is it? For one thing, it is an undeclared war, and perhaps more important, it is war without end, without final surrender or meaningful victory. It is not like the American Civil War, or the two world wars the United States was involved in. A better parallel would be the Cold War, which like the war on terrorism is more a metaphor than the real thing. Yet both the Cold War and the current continuing war against terrorism are warlike in their effects on governments and populations. Under the threat of imminent attack, both governments and populations are ready to go into war mode, militarizing the entire tone of daily life and of governmental policy.[19] In a state of continuing alert and fear, populations are willing to see government powers expand and social resources mobilized in defense of the nation. This is what gave rise to the institutions and instruments of what would become known as the surveillance state, or the national security state, or, more flippantly, the warfare state. They coalesced into the enduring structures of what we can no longer meaningfully call a state of exception. Many of the war-mode strategic and tactical responses that the Bush and Obama administrations have come up with are, on closer inspection, no more than elaborations on themes well established since early Cold War days. Those were the days when America first became aware of its position of hegemon in the world, a position that—as the Greek etymology of the word suggests—asked for leadership and dominance. Those were the days when American leadership first implied the projection of an imperial view of the world, giving a global cast to the emerging Cold War conflict.

Shaping its role, America engaged in developing the panoply of tools it needed for deploying its power. Many were visible and aboveboard, like building up a war arsenal, developing new weapons, setting up military alliances. All this went to structure its empire, its power reach, and to define the perimeter of its area of hegemony. Yet drawing on lessons learned during two real wars, World War I and World War II, in the manner of a new state of exception, the United States morphed into invisible forms of government. In their 1964 book *The Invisible Government,* the authors, David Wise and Thomas B. Ross, caused a shock from its very first paragraph: "There are two governments in the United States today. One is visible. The other invisible." The authors continued: "The first is the government that citizens read about in their newspapers and children study about in their civics books. The second is the interlocking, hidden machinery that carries out the policies of the United States in the Cold War. This second, invisible government gathers intelligence, conducts espionage, and plans and executes secret operations all over the globe."[20] By 1964 the U.S. Intelligence Community, or IC, had nine members, including the CIA, the Defense Intelligence Agency (DIA), and the National Security Agency (NSA). As Wise and Ross portrayed it, the IC was already a labyrinthine set of secret outfits with growing power. It was capable of launching covert actions worldwide, with a "broad spectrum of domestic operations," the ability to overthrow foreign governments, if need be through political assassinations, and the capacity to plan operations without the knowledge of Congress or full presidential control. "No outsider is in a position to determine whether or not, in time, these activities might become an internal danger to a free society."[21] By 2012 the IC, with seventeen official outfits, had almost doubled. The internal danger they jointly pose has grown incommensurably larger. With the latest technology of data gathering and data mining, massive flows of communication between individuals within the realm are now continually being stored and analyzed, without proper oversight, without means of legal recourse for individual citizens.

This invisible government has surrounded itself with a wall of secrecy, jealously and vindictively protected from whistleblowers through the revival of dormant antiespionage legislation. The 1917 Espionage Act, duly enacted by Congress at a time of real war, during a real "state of exception," and never used since, is now dusted off and has been used on several occasions by the Obama administration. When the state of exception has become the "new normal," civil oversight of government actions has become a distant dream. Exposing patent war crimes through channels such as Wikileaks, or the rise of a surveillance state through the massive leaks by Edward Snowden, has now become a crime itself.

All this is reminiscent of an earlier episode, in the post-Watergate years, when an emerging imperial presidency found its check and balance in a Congress eager to regain its constitutional role. The Pentagon Papers case was thrown out of court for miscarriage of justice. Hearings by the Church Committee brought secrets of the "invisible government," as it had been shaping up during the Cold War, to light. Congressional powers were restored, as in the War Powers Act. CIA ventures in the area of political assassination were stopped as being illegal, unwarranted by claims of war-connected states of exception.

The long history of the imperial presidency has resumed its irresistible course since. If assassinations as an instrument of covert foreign policy had been proscribed in the 1970s, extrajudicial killing by the U.S. government has now become routine, an acceptable tool in the war against terrorism, a war with no end in sight. The state of exception proclaimed in connection to that war, a connection emphasized in legal memos for the government and in the few public accounts given by government officials, has now come to define the "new normal." Exception has become the rule.[22]

The constant surveillance of human interactions and exchanges within the reach of America's empire, the deployment of military force through a network of interlinked bases, the walls of secrecy surrounding it all, form today's U.S. invisible government.[23] It is a government that in its own inner logic makes for one, undivided center of command and control. It is the inexorable logic that I earlier gave the name of the imperial imperative. It exerts its compelling force on whoever holds the office of president and commander-in-chief, the person in charge of both the visible and invisible government. Juggling both roles of elected chief executive and guardian of national security under conditions of war, presidents have come to stretch the limits of states of exception to the point where the exception becomes the rule. If we still need a definition of American exceptionalism, this may be it.

[10]

TAKING EXCEPTION

IN A NATIONALLY televised speech on Syria, on Tuesday night, September 10, 2013, Obama turned to American exceptionalism as a call to action for an endeavor in which his country stood isolated in the world. "America is not the world's policeman. Terrible things happen across the globe, and it is beyond our means to right every wrong," Obama said. "But when, with modest effort and risk, we can stop children from being gassed to death, and thereby make our own children safer over the long run, I believe we should act." He added: "That's what makes America different. That's what makes us exceptional." The concluding word must have brought a wry smile to some at least among his listeners. They must have recognized its use not as powerful rhetoric, to clinch the argument, but rather as formulaic, as a shibboleth granting safe passage to a man whose political credentials had never been fully accepted by a vengeful part of the American citizenry. The word "exceptional" had become the litmus test to those in the media and the political arena who were out to deconstruct and undermine the president from the moment he had entered office.

Obama may have quickly learned his lesson, paying tribute, if not lip service, to a word that was of relatively recent currency in American political discourse. The role it played, though, was like that of earlier passwords, such as "Americanism" and "anticommunism," as in the days of the Red Scare following World War I or in the early years of the Cold War with McCarthyism in the role of monitor and protector of the purity of the body politic. The monitoring gaze this time comes once again from the political right, embodied in its lunatic fringe of the Tea Party.

Yet it would be wrong to see Obama as merely paying lip service to the word "exceptionalism" and all it stands for in summary of a larger American creed. Many have been the occasions, from his early presidency on, where we can see Obama revisiting the concept, not just to pay tribute and be done with it, but to consider the options it gave him to be an educator of the nation, to bring a degree of subtlety, nuance, and complexity to a word that too often was used as a facile trope. The way Obama used the word was very much in the vein of what Sacvan Bercovitch has called the American Jeremiad, a particular use of public speech that reminds the audience of its high calling while pointing to the many ways in which it is still remiss, falling short.[1] Listen to Obama, in 2008:

> We have a core set of values that are enshrined in our Constitution, in our body of law, in our democratic practices, in our belief in free speech and equality, that, though imperfect, are exceptional.
>
> Now, the fact that I am very proud of my country and I think that we've got a whole lot to offer the world does not lessen my interest in recognizing the value and wonderful qualities of other countries, or recognizing that we're not always going to be right, or that other people may have good ideas, or that in order for us to work collectively, all parties have to compromise and that includes us.
>
> I see no contradiction between believing that America has a continued extraordinary role in leading the world toward peace and prosperity and recognizing that leadership is incumbent, depends

on, our ability to create partnerships because we can't solve these problems alone.

In the eyes of the monitoring right, qualifying words like "though imperfect," or the call for compromise, while acknowledging that other people may have good ideas, may already be far too subtle and nuanced. But what caused them to rise in howling anger were Obama's opening words—often the only words quoted in the right's indictment: "I believe in American exceptionalism, just as I suspect that Brits believe in British exceptionalism and the Greeks believe in Greek exceptionalism." As right-wing commentator Michael Barone thundered: "One cannot imagine Presidents Roosevelt, Truman or Kennedy, Eisenhower or Reagan, uttering such sentiments."[2] Up against such odds, a man like Obama, politician and intellectual, has to tack to political winds while keeping an eye on the compass of his convictions. He has kept valiantly trying to add a touch of realism and relativism to the idea of American exceptionalism, much as that very endeavor is an abomination in the eyes of the Tea Party watch dogs. To those with a historian's memory, however, it may even appear as if Obama has been trying to add an almost European sense of the fallibility and frailty of human exploits to counter the more impetuous uses of exceptionalism in American political discourse. I for one could not help being reminded of C. Vann Woodward's reading of the historical experience of the American post–Civil War South as the only region in the United States to have experienced defeat and loss and to have developed a quasi-European sense of the tragic.[3] Some of that sobering sense, I feel, is what Obama is struggling to convey to a larger American public.

There is a further irony here. If my reading of the gist of Obama's revisits of the concept of exceptionalism is correct, it would highlight a resemblance between his aims and current trends in the academic study of the United States. What C. Vann Woodward had still to call a counterpoint to the prevailing mainstream reading of American history in his day has now become a widespread inspiration in the fields of American history and American Studies. The urge began to be felt from the 1990s onward to break out of a conceptual view of America as sui generis, as exceptional, as different in its historical experience and destiny than any other country in the world. For one thing, this sense could inspire an exploration of the many ways in which the United States had proved different than other countries, though not exceptional. The best encyclopedic treatment is Seymour Martin Lipset's *American Exceptionalism*.[4] A comparativist, Lipset looked at a number of areas in political and social life where the United States traditionally had been seen as forming an exception to rules prevalent in Europe. Thus he revisited Tocqueville's aperçus concerning the lasting effects of America's special historical genesis and development, and the German early-twentieth-century historian and sociologist Werner Sombart's classic study on the question of why there is no socialism in the United States. They are all areas where America can be seen to offer counterpoints to European history while in other areas it moved in step with European history. Thus America could be woven into a larger narrative of forces of social change and modernization as these affected nations on both sides of the Atlantic, each with its own peculiar quirks and twists. Yet it has taken more than a little pushing to shatter the hold of exceptionalism on American historiography.

In an influential essay, entitled "Exceptionalism," Daniel Rodgers made the point that from the early modern era to the postcolonial present, the cultivation of sentiments of difference and superiority has been at the heart of the project of nation-state formation. Within these common terms, however, there has run a thread that, if not wholly distinct to the American complex, carries there a peculiarly striking weight. That is the idea of exceptionalism. Rodgers then makes the following simple but crucial point: exceptionalism differs from difference. Difference requires contrast; exceptionalism requires a rule. Exceptionalist claims pin one's own nation's distinctiveness to every other people's sameness—to general laws and conditions governing everything but the special case at hand. When difference is put in exceptionalist terms, the exception becomes an exemption, an exemption from the universal tendencies of history, the "normal" fate of nations, the laws of historical mechanics itself.[5]

It is implications like these, where a nation can claim to be above the general rule, if not above the law, that have inspired America's political action as much as its self-reflection. If other nations have agreed to set up an International Criminal Court, America is no party to it, refusing to abide by rules that others have subjected themselves to. Yet among American academics strong movements have occurred to do away with exceptionalism in their understanding of the driving forces behind American history. Programs aiming at "transnationalizing" or globalizing the intellectual paradigms of American history and American Studies found wide support in the main professional organizations. Daniel Rodgers published a pioneering study, entitled *Atlantic Crossings*, that illustrated the gains to be had from internationalizing the frame of interpretation. *Atlantic Crossings* is the first major account of the vibrant international network that American reformers, Progressives, and, later, New Dealers constructed and of its profound impact on the United States from the 1870s through 1945, a story so often obscured by notions of American exceptionalism.[6] At about the same time two collections of essays were published with the broad support of the Organization of American Historians (OAH), edited respectively by David Thelen and Thomas Bender.[7] Both publishing projects broadly aimed at questioning the nation-centered focus of American history, as Thelen has it, or as Bender puts it: "To historicize the nation is to relate its dominant narrative, its national narrative, to other narratives that refer to both smaller histories and larger ones. That means understanding the historical production of the nation and locating it in a context larger than itself."[8]

Words like "the historical production of the nation" betray an affinity and intellectual exchange with yet another community of students of America, those active in the intellectual domain of a self-styled American Studies. Always more open to intellectual perspectives current among cultural studies scholars, more willing to use a language that emphasizes the constructionist elements of reality, of reality as imagined and agreed on through social interactions, American Studies people set upon the "deconstruction" of their own academic field with a vengeance. At times it showed a vehemence as if the issue was a matter of exorcism, of driving out all the evil connotations of the word "America," in an act of linguistic voluntarism, as if changing the language one used would change the world. It led one outsider to scathingly speak of Anti-American Studies, in a facetious review in the *New Republic* of three examples of the new postexceptionalist American Studies.[9]

It was not long, though, before sobering second thoughts came to some of the leading "New Americanists." In a piece entitled "Re-thinking 'American Studies after U.S. Exceptionalism,'" Donald Pease acknowledged the resistance to change of large swaths of reality. "Transnational American Studies aspired to remediate the discourse of U.S. exceptionalism by transnationalizing the core values of American civil society. But global civil society has neither transcended the era of the nation-state nor entered into the utopian realm of a cosmopolitan democracy. Have not scholars in transnational American Studies overestimated the ways in which global civil society can mobilize the political energies needed to remedy the economic inequalities that globalization has engendered? Has not post-exceptionalist American Studies also ignored the U.S. state's power to describe the U.S. as a permanent state of exception?"[10] There is a remarkable return here, linked undoubtedly to the aftermath of 9/11 and the American display of what is known among military people as "full spectrum dominance," to age-old concepts like the state and the state's power, or for that matter the nation-state and its attendant nationalism. The permanent state of exception ironically is presented here as a product of the state's power, as the outcome of the state's power to manipulate reality for its citizenry. We mentioned linguistic voluntarism before, but if one needs proof of it happening, here it is.

Clearly the work of "re-mapping the trans-national"—the name of the series in which this book appears—is a work in progress. How do I see the place of my book in the larger project? For one thing, for much of my life as an academic active in American Studies at the University of Amsterdam, the Netherlands, one continuing theme has been my study of the many ways in which American and European cultures have cross-pollinated and the ways in which cultural influences were received or resisted. Part of my interest there was in issues of Americanization of European cultures or of European anti-Americanism, on either political or cultural grounds. Some chapters in this book clearly reflect that interest, while also critically revisiting it, particularly the chapter on "Cool Hand Luck." If issues of empire and imperial sway show up in my writing there, it is clearly in response to wider intellectual concerns in the post-9/11 study of America. Issues of politics and power have forced themselves upon my mind most directly in the opening and concluding chapters of the book, on the George W. Bush administration first, on the Obama administration later. The chapters were written against the backdrop of general mood-swings, both in the United States and in Europe. There is one more general aspect of transnationalism, though, that I only became aware of while writing the book. In my earlier writing on American popular culture in particular I tried to answer questions as to what accounts for the lure and appeal of American popular culture, at home and abroad. In this book, though, I found that my interest had moved to the darker side of popular culture and forms of entertainment, even in such gruesome varieties as lynchings. I also found, more clearly than ever before, that there are forms of transnationalism inherent to the train of thought of the human mind. Writing about freaks in 1930s America, and the Lilliput town on Long Island that housed them, styled after the German medieval city of Nurnberg, brought images to my mind of Nazi Germany and its persecution of freaks. Images of the Nazi holocaust called up pictures in my mind of photographs as they had circulated in the United States. What I am trying to say, is that the transnationalism that one can see happening here is almost like a chimera, one image shimmering through another one, as if in a palimpsest. History does form palimpsests, covering one layer of images with later ones, as if on the wall of an old house with one painted advertisement not quite covering a preceding one. It is an uncanny experience if, by looking intently at one image, another one shows up, shimmering through, taking one from one locale and time to another. It is also exhilarating.

NOTES

Introduction

1. See www.huffingtonpost.com/pierre-guerlain/democracy-in-america-it -w_b_4077088.html.

2. Michelle Alexander, *The New Jim Crow: Mass Incarceration in the Age of Color Blindness* (New York: New Press, 2010); *Report of the Sentencing Project to the United Nations Human Rights Committee Regarding Racial Disparities in the United States Criminal Justice System* (Washington, DC: The Sentencing project, Research and Advocacy for Reform, August 2013), http://sentencingproject.org/doc/publications/rd_ICCPR%20Race% 20and%20Justice%20Shadow%20Report.pdf.

3. Samuel Bowles and Arjun Jayadev, "One Nation under Guard," http:// opinionator.blogs.nytimes.com/2014/02/15/one-nation-under-guard/?_ php=true&_type=blogs&_r=0.

4. *Runaway Train* is a 1985 American film, directed by Andrei Konchalovsky. The screenplay by Djordje Milicevic, Paul Zindel, and Edward Bunker was based on an original screenplay by Akira Kurosawa with uncredited contributions by frequent Kurosawa collaborators Hideo Oguni and Ryuzo Kikushima. It stars Jon Voight, Eric Roberts, Rebecca De Mornay and John P. Ryan. © 1985 Cannon Films, Inc.

5. Quoted in Jackson Lears, "Editor's Note," *Raritan: A Quarterly Review* (Summer 2013).

Chapter 1. The George W. Bush Administration and European Anti-Americanism

This text originates in my retirement address delivered at the University of Amsterdam. It captures the sense of alienation of a European Americanist at the time of the George W. Bush administration. The original version was published by the *Journal of American History* 93, no. 2 (September 2006): 417–32. It was entitled "European Anti-Americanism: What's New?"

1. Jean-Marie Colombani, "Nous sommes tous Américains," *Le Monde* (Paris), September 13, 2001, 1; Thomas Jefferson, "First Inaugural Address," March 4, 1801, in *Inaugural Addresses of the Presidents of the United States from George Washington 1789 to George Bush 1989*, comp. Joint Congressional Committee on Inaugural Ceremonies (Washington, DC, 1989), 101–10.

2. President George H. W. Bush used the phrase in his September 11, 1990, address to a joint session of Congress, http:/en.wikisource.org/wiki/Toward_a_New_World_Order.

3. On this topic, see Jaap Kooijman, "Bombs Bursting in Air: The Gulf War, 9/11, and the Super Bowl Performances of 'The Star-Spangled Banner' by Whitney Houston and Mariah Carey," in Ruud Janssens and Rob Kroes, eds., *Post-Cold War Europe, Post-Cold War America* (Amsterdam: VU University Press, 2004), 178–94.

4. Richard Rorty, "Post-Democracy," *London Review of Books* (April 1, 2004). In a spirited response, as yet unpublished, Tomas Mastnak, currently a fellow at the International Center for Advanced Studies at New York University, took Rorty to task for ignoring recent trends in the United States.

5. "Secretary Rumsfeld Briefs at the Foreign Press Center," press brief, January 22, 2003, U.S. Department of Defense, http://www.dod.gov/transcripts/2003/t01232003_t0122sdfpc.html.

6. Alfred Grosser, "Les hors-la-loi," *Le Monde,* Friday, April 18, 2003, reprinted in *Le Monde, Sélection hebdomadaire* no. 2842 (April 26, 2003): 8.

7. At this point it may suffice to refer the reader to my earlier work on the topic, in *If You've Seen One, You've Seen the Mall: Europeans and American Mass Culture* (Chicago: University of Illinois Press, 1996), ch. 1; and *Them and Us: Questions of Citizenship in a Globalizing World* (University of Illinois Press, 2000), ch. 9. See also Philippe Roger, *The American Enemy: The History of French Anti-Americanism* (Chicago: University of Chicago Press, 2005).

8. The words "agonizing reappraisal" were used by John Foster Dulles on December 14, 1953, when he said in Paris that if the French Assembly did not approve the European Defense Community treaty, "that would compel an agonizing reappraisal" of basic U.S. foreign policy toward France.

9. Michael Ignatieff, "What We Think of America," *Granta* 77 (Spring 2002): 47–50.

10. In an interview in the *Guardian* on August 27, 2003.

11. *Guardian Weekly*, May 28–June 3, 2004, 7.

12. Quoted in Michael Massing, "Unfit to Print?" *New York Review of Books* 55, 11 (June 24, 2004): 8.

13. Ibid., 10.

14. See, for example, the chapter "America and the World as America," in Ziauddin Sardar and Merryl Wyn Davies, *Why Do People Hate America?* (Cambridge: ICON Books, 2002). Similar best-selling indictments, in languages other than English, of America's recent course in world politics and the failure of the American press to take an independent and critical position are, for example, Hans Leyendecker, *Die Lügen des Weissen Hauses: Warum Amerika einen Neuanfang braucht* [The Lies of the White House: Why America Needs a New Start] (Reinbek bei Hamburg: Rowohlt, 2004); Karel van Wolferen, *De ondergang van een wereldorde* [The Demise of a World Order] (Amsterdam: Uitgeverij Contact, 2003); and Denise Artaud, *L'Amérique des néoconservateurs: L'Empire a-t-il un avenir?* [The America of the Neo-Conservatives: Has the Empire a Future?] (Paris: Editions Ellipses, 2004).

15. Philip Knightley, "Losing Friends and Influencing People," *Index on Censorship* 31, 1 (January 2002): 146–55.

16. Ronald L. Inglehart, ed., *Human Values and Social Change: Findings from the Values Surveys,* International Studies in Sociology and Social Anthropology, vol. 89 (The Hague: Brill, 2002).

17. See Ira Chernus, www.tomdispatch.com/index.mhtml?pid=2068.

18. I may refer the reader to my survey of such French views of American modernity. See Kroes, *Them and Us,* ch. 9.

19. See, for example, Annick Foucrier, *Le rêve californien: Migrants francais sur la côte Pacifique (XVIIIe–XXe siècles)* (Paris: Belin, 1999).

20. See Kroes, *If You've Seen One, You've Seen the Mall.*

21. Quoted in D. Lacorne, J. Rupnik, and M. F. Toinet, eds., *L'Amérique dans les têtes* (Paris: Hachette, 1986), 61.

22. Quoted in ibid., 62.

23. Robert Kagan, *Of Paradise and Power: America and Europe in the New World Order* (New York: Alfred A. Knopf, 2003).

24. Larry Siedentop, *Democracy in Europe* (London: Penguin Books, 2000), 190, 195, 198.

25. I am paraphrasing the comic Rob Corddry on *The Daily Show with Jon Stewart*: "It's our principles that matter, our inspiring, abstract notions. Remember: Just because torturing prisoners is something we did, [that] doesn't mean it's something we *would* do." Quoted by Mark Danner in his "The Logic of Torture," *New York Review of Books* 51, 11 (June 24, 2004): 74.

26. *Süddeutsche Zeitung* 138 (June 18, 2004): 15.

27. J. Habermas, *Der gespaltete Westen* (Frankfurt am Main: Suhrkamp Verlag, 2004). The quotation is from the interview in the *Süddeutsche Zeitung.*

28. *Le Monde Sélection Hebdomadaire*, May 22, 2004. The French caption reads: "Tous non-américains?"

Chapter 2. The Ascent of the Falling Man:
An Iconic Image of 9/11

This piece has evolved from passages in my *Photographic Memories: Private Pictures, Public Images, and American History* (Hanover, NH: University Press of New England, 2007). Ever since I have been trying to translate into language my continuing fascination with one particular image among the flood of visual material produced by 9/11. The piece has benefited greatly from critical comments by colleagues and friends, in particular Geoffrey Batchen, Kate Delaney, Mick Gidley, Jay Prosser, Derek Rubin, Robert Rydell, and Jaap Verheul.

1. Albert Boime, "The Fate of the Image-Monument in the Wake of 9/11," in Vincent Lavoie, ed., *NOW: Images of Present Time* (Montreal: Le Mois de la Photo à Montréal, 2003), 189–204.

2. Alain Mons, *La traversée du visible: Images et lieux du contemporain* (Paris: Les Editions de la Passion, 2002), 32 (my translation).

3. Ibid., 30.

4. In a piece tellingly titled "Still Life," Laura Frost addresses the issue of, as her subtitle has it, "9/11's Falling Bodies." She recognizes photography's inherent power to make time stand still, a power that inspired Polish poet Wislawa Szymrska. See Laura Frost, "Still Life: 9/11's Falling Bodies," in Ann Keniston and Jeanne Follansbee Quinn, eds., *Literature after 9/11* (London: Routledge, 2008), 180–207.

5. Walter Benjamin, "The Work of Art in the Age of Mechanical Reproduction," in *Illuminations* (New York: Schocken, 1969), 236–37.

6. Don DeLillo, *Falling Man* (New York: Scribner, 2007), 168.

7. Ibid., 221–22.

8. The firefighter is shown in the documentary film *9/11*, produced by Jules and Gédéon Naudet, two French documentary filmmakers who happened to be in New York making a film about one rookie firefighter who underwent his fire baptism on the day of 9/11. The film contains gripping footage from inside one of the burning towers, but likewise makes a stated conscious choice not to *show* the falling bodies. Instead, one hears the *thud* of their hitting the ground. *9/11, A Film by Jules and Gédéon Naudet and James Hanlon* (Goldfish Pictures, Inc., 2001).

9. Ric Burns, *New York: The Center of the World, A Documentary Film* (Boston: WGBH, 2003), Episode Eight: 1946–2003.

10. Tom Junod, "The Falling Man," *Esquire* 140, 3 (September 2003): 177–78.

11. See www.newsday.com/news/nationaworld/wire/la-oe-drew10sep10, 0,2008868.story?coll=sns-ap-nationworld-headlines.

12. Junod, "The Falling Man."

13. *9/11: The Falling Man* (directed by Henry Singer, filmed by Richard Nemeroff, using Lyle Owerko's photographs of falling people. First aired on British television network *Channel 4*, 2006). The film is available on two websites: www.youtube.com/watch?v=BXnA9FjvLSU; and http://video .google.com/videoplay?docid=-1643316699854377441#.

14. Words quoted from the documentary *9/11: The Falling Man*. The theme of the ethnic response to 9/11 photographs, and to the Falling Man in particular, I have explored more fully in my "Indecent Exposure: Picturing the Horror of 9/11," in Derek Rubin and Jaap Verheul, eds., *American Multiculturalism after 9/11: Transatlantic Perspectives* (Amsterdam: Amsterdam University Press, 2009), 67–81.

15. One site in particular devotes itself to the memory of those who perished on 9/11: www.september11victims.com/september11victims/Victim Info.asp?ID=1345.

16. Jonathan Safran Foer, *Extremely Loud and Incredibly Close* (New York: Houghton, Mifflin, Harcourt, 2005).

17. Devin Zuber, "Flanerie at Ground Zero: Aesthetic Countermemories in Lower Manhattan," *American Quarterly* 58, 2 (2006): 269–99.

18. Art Spiegelman, *In the Shadow of No Towers* (New York: Pantheon Books, 2004).

19. "Postmemory" is a term suggested by Marianne Hirsch in her *Family Frames: Photography, Narrative and Postmemory* (Cambridge: Harvard University Press, 1997). It describes the sort of memory that people form of past events they have not directly witnessed.

20. Kristiaan Versluys, "9/11 in the Novel," in Matthew J. Morgan, ed., *The Impact of 9/11 on the Media, Arts, and Entertainment: The Day That Changed Everything?* (London: Palgrave Macmillan, 2009), 142–43.

Chapter 3. Cool Hand Luck: How America Played Its Hand Entertaining the World

WORKS CITED

Barlow, Joel. An oration: delivered at the North Church in Hartford,
    at the meeting of the Connecticut Society of the Cincinnati, July 4,

1787. In commemoration of the independence of the United States (Hartford: Hudson and Goodwin, 1787).

Baudrillard, Jean. *La Guerre du Golfe n'a pas eu lieu*. Paris: Galilée, 1991.

———. *The Gulf War Did Not Take Place*. Trans. Paul Patton. Bloomington: Indiana University Press, 2005.

Croly, Herbert. *The Promise of American Life*. New York: Macmillan, 1909.

De Grazia, Victoria. *Irresistible Empire: America's Advance through Twentieth-Century Europe*. Cambridge: Harvard University Press, 2005.

Foreign Affair. Dir. Billy Wilder. Writ. Charles Brackett et al. Perf. Jean Arthur, Marlene Dietrich, and John Lund. USA: Paramount Pictures, 1948.

Fulbright, J. William. "The Arrogance of Power." Christian A. Herter lecture, delivered at Johns Hopkins University, Spring 1966. See www.h-net.org/~hst306/documents/fulbright.html. Last accessed August 16, 2012.

Kaplan, Amy. "Violent Belongings and the Question of Empire Today." *American Quarterly* 56, 1 (March 1994): 1–18.

Kings of the Road [Im Laufe der Zeit]. Dir. Wim Wenders. Writ. Wim Wenders. Perf. Rüdiger Vogler, Hanns Zischler, and Lisa Kreuzer. West Germany: Wim Wenders Productions, 1976.

Leuchtenburg, William E. "Progressivism and Imperialism: The Progressive Movement and American Foreign Policy, 1898–1916." *Mississippi Valley Historical Review* 39, 3 (December 1952): 483–504.

Maier, Charles S. *Among Empires: American Ascendency and Its Predecessors*. Cambridge: Harvard University Press, 2007.

Man Who Shot Liberty Valance. Dir. John Ford. Writ. James Warner Bellah et al. Perf. James Stewart, John Wayne, and Vera Miles. USA: Paramount Pictures, 1962.

Menand, Louis. "The Promise of Freedom, the Friend of Authority: American Culture in Postwar France." In Michael Kazin and Joseph A. McCartin, eds., *Americanism: New Perspectives on the History of an Ideal*. Chapel Hill: University of North Carolina Press, 2006, 205–20.

Muguruza, Fermin. "Big Beñat." Dir. Telmo Esnal and Asier Altuna. See www.youtube.com/watch?v=OXuffvjs_Ps. Last accessed November 29, 2012.

Pease, Donald E., and Robyn Wiegman, eds. *The Futures of American Studies*. Durham, NC: Duke University Press, 2002.

Puya, feat. Connect-r. "My Americandrim." Dir. Marian Crisan. Roma-

nia: Scandalos Music, 2010. See www.youtube.com/watch?v=xGt
lounpxm8. Last accessed August 16, 2012.

Radway, Janice A. "What's in a Name? Presidential Address to the
American Studies Association, November 20, 1998." *American
Quarterly* 51, 1 (March 1999): 1–32.

Robertson, Roland. "Globalisation or Glocalisation?" *Journal of International Communication* 1, 1 (1994): 33–52.

Rydell, R. W., and Rob Kroes. *Buffalo Bill in Bologna: The Americanization
of the World, 1869–1922*. Chicago: Chicago University Press, 2005.

Suskind, Ron. "Faith, Certainty and the Presidency of George W. Bush."
New York Times Magazine (October 17, 2004). See www.nytimes.com/
2004/10/17/magazine/17BUSH.html. Last accessed August 16, 2012.

1. For a classic elaboration of the concept of a democracy of goods, see
Roland Marchand, *Advertising the American Dream: Making Way for Modernity,1920–1940* (Berkeley: University of California Press, 1985). See also
Lisabeth Cohen, *A Consumers' Republic: The Politics of Mass Consumption
in Postwar America* (New York: Knopf, 2003).

2. Compare Louis Menand, "The Promise of Freedom, the Friend of Au-
thority: American Culture in Postwar France," in Michael Kazin and Joseph
A. McCartin, eds., *Americanism: New Perspectives on the History of an
Ideal* (Chapel Hill: University of North Carolina Press, 2006), 213.

3. In my *If You've Seen One, You've Seen the Mall: Europeans and American Mass Culture* (Chicago: University of Illinois Press, 1996), I give many
examples for a range of European countries, for the post–World War I period, particularly chapters 1 and 3.

4. It is interesting to contrast this music video with one produced more
recently in Romania, by singer Puya, featuring Connect-r, called "Americandrim" (American Dream). Against the backdrop of contemporary Romania,
presented as a landscape of broken dreams with its democratic promise unfulfilled, the singer conjures up one tempting element after another of an
imaginary America, as it feeds his dreams of "losing his identity, becoming
an American." Clearly, in different parts of contemporary Europe, America
still plays a number of roles, from tempting model to baneful force of alienation and dehumanization.

5. Ron Suskind, "Faith, Certainty and the Presidency of George W. Bush,"
New York Times Magazine, October 17, 2004, www.nytimes.com/2004/10
/17/magazine/17BUSH.html (last accessed July 14, 2014).

6. For "empire of liberty," see Robert W. Tucker and David C. Hendrick-

son, *Empire of Liberty: The Statecraft of Thomas Jefferson* (New York: Oxford University Press, 1990). The words "empire of reason" are from a statement in an oration on July 4, 1787, by Joel Barlow at Hartford, Connecticut, in celebration of the anniversary of the proclamation of the Declaration of Independence: "The present is an age of philosophy, and America the empire of reason. Here, neither the pageantry of courts, nor the glooms of superstition, have dazzled or beclouded the mind. Our duty calls us to act worthy of the age and the country that gave us birth. Though inexperience may have betrayed us into errors—yet they have not been fatal: and our own discernment will point us to their proper remedy."

7. In the spring of 1966, Senator Fulbright delivered the Christian A. Herter Lecture at Johns Hopkins University on the arrogance of power. For the full speech, see www.h-net.org/~hst306/documents/fulbright.html. The same year, Fulbright published his book *The Arrogance of Power*, in which he analyzed U.S.-American foreign policy and criticized the justifications for the Vietnam War.

8. On the early formation of American mass culture, see R. W. Rydell and Rob Kroes, *Buffalo Bill in Bologna: The Americanization of the World, 1869–1922* (2005).

9. A seminal publication blazing the trail for the new American Studies is Donald E. Pease, Jr., and Robyn Wiegman, eds., *The Futures of American Studies* (2002).

10. Amy Kaplan, "Violent Belongings and the Question of Empire Today," *Presidential Address to the American Studies Association*, Hartford, CT, October 17, 2003, American Quarterly 56, 1 (March 2004): 1–18.

11. Among the works that Kaplan so astutely summarizes here, one stands out for its dispassionate positioning of America among its imperial predecessors: Charles S. Maier, *Among Empires: American Ascendency and Its Predecessors* (2007).

12. Kaplan, "Violent Belongings and the Question of Empire Today," 2.

13. A classic piece is by William E. Leuchtenburg, "Progressivism and Imperialism: The Progressive Movement and American Foreign Policy, 1898–1916" (1952).

Chapter 4. Musical America: Staging the U.S.A.
to the Sounds of Music

1. Thus, the February 1, 1893, *New York Times*, under the heading "Henry Smith Lynching Victim," reported: "Another Negro burned; Henry Smith dies at the stake" before going into gruesome detail.

2. Alex Ross, *The Rest Is Noise: Listening to the Twentieth Century* (New York: Farrar, Straus and Giroux, 2007), 127.

3. David A. Hollinger, *Postethnic America: Beyond Multiculturalism* (New York: Basic Books, 1995, 2000).

4. Arthur M. Schlesinger, *The Disuniting of America: Reflections on a Multicultural Society* (New York: W. W. Norton and Company, 1991).

5. Ross, *The Rest Is Noise,* 150.

6. As told by Trevor Nunn, director of the Glyndebourne production, in the PBS television documentary "Porgy and Bess: An American Voice," www.pbs.org/wnet/gperf/porgy/.

7. See http://movies.nytimes.com/movie/review?res=9B05E3DF103FEE3 BBC4D52DFB366838D629EDE.

8. See www.bbc.co.uk/iplayer/episode/b03fvds9/Arena_Arena_The_National_Theatre_Part_Two_War_and_Peace/.

9. Roland Robertson, "Glocalization: Time-Space and Homogeneity-Heterogeneity," in M. Featherstone, S. Lash, and R. Robertson, eds. Global Modernities (London: Sage, 1995), 25–44.

10. See www.youtube.com/watch?v=OXuffvjs_Ps (song and lyrics by Fermin Muguruza).

11. See www.youtube.com/watch?v=RFKa_gaFMlQ (song and lyrics by Puya and Connect-R).

Chapter 5. A Spaghetti Southern: Landscapes of Fear in Quentin Tarantino's Django Unchained

1. Leslie A. Fiedler, *The Return of the Vanishing American* (New York: Stein and Day, 1968).

2. Norman Mailer, "The White Negro: Superficial Reflections on the Hipster," *Dissent* (Fall 1957).

3. William Faulkner, *Absalom, Absalom!* (1936; New York: Random House, 1964), 174.

4. Louis Menand, "The Promise of Freedom, the Friend of Authority: American Culture in Postwar France," in Michael Kazin and Joseph A. McCartin, eds., *Americanism: New Perspectives on the History of an Ideal* (Chapel Hill: University of North Carolina Press, 2006), 213–14.

5. Nino Frank, "A New Kind of Police Drama: The Criminal Adventure," (1946) in Alain Silver and James Ursini, eds., *Film Noir Reader* 2 (New York: Limelight, 1999).

6. *Alphaville, une étrange aventure de Lemmy Caution* (dir. Jean-Luc Godard, 1965).

7. John G. Blair, "Cowboys, Europe and Smoke: Marlboro in the Saddle," in Rob Kroes, ed., *The American West as Seen by Europeans and Americans* (Amsterdam: Free University Press, 1989), 360–84.

8. I purposefully use Joseph Conrad's metaphor of the heart of darkness. In fact, like Conrad, Tarantino uses a narrative trope that has much older roots. Like precursors from classical antiquity, such as Odysseus or Orpheus descending into Hades—a trope known as "katabasis," or "Nekuia"—often with the point of retrieving loved ones, Django has set out on a similar mission.

9. Enzo Barboni, "Lo Chiamavano Trinità," 1970.

10. David Denby, "Tarantino's Crap Masterpiece, 'Django Unchained': Put-On, Revenge, and the Aesthetics of Trash," *New Yorker,* January 22, 2013, www.newyorker.com/online/blogs/culture/2013/01/django-unchained -reviewed-tarantinos-crap-masterpiece.html.

11. "Quentin Tarantino: I'm proud of my flop," www.telegraph.co.uk /culture/film/starsandstories/3664742/Quentin-Tarantino-Im-proud-of-my -flop.html.

12. See http://insidemovies.ew.com/2012/07/14/django-unchained-comic -con-panel-tarantino-talks-links-to-other-movies-don-johnson-talks-fog horn-leghorn/.

13. Sandy Alexandre, *The Properties of Violence: Claims to Ownership in Representations of Lynching* (Jackson: University Press of Mississippi, 2012), 193.

14. Ibid.

15. Ibid.

16. James Allen et al., *Without Sanctuary: Lynching Photography in America* (Santa Fe, NM: Twin Palms Publishers, 2000).

17. Mamie Till Bradley and Christopher Benson, *Death of Innocence: The Story of the Hate Crime That Changed America* (New York: Random House, 2003), 98, 114.

18. On this aspect, see Stephen J. Whitfield, *A Death in the Delta: The Story of Emmett Till* (Baltimore, MD: Johns Hopkins University Press, 1991), 18.

Chapter 6. Freaks on Display: A Tale of Empathy and Ostracism

1. Leslie A. Fiedler, *Freaks: Myths and Images of the Secret Self* (New York: Simon and Schuster, 1978).

2. The album cover for *Diamond Dogs* was designed by Belgian artist Guy Peellaert. Compare Ian Buruma, "The Invention of David Bowie," *New*

York Review of Books (May 23, 2013): 8–12. On the case of Michael Jackson, see "Dancing with the Elephant Man's Bones: A Star Study of Michael Jackson," ch. V in Raphael Raphael, *The New American Grotesque: Freaks and Other Monstrous and Extraordinary Bodies* (unpublished dissertation, University of Oregon, June 2009).

3. Susan M. Schweick, *The Ugly Laws: Disability in Public* (New York: New York University Press, 2009).

4. Tanfer Emin Tunç, "Freaks and Geeks: Coney Island Sideshow Performers and Long Island Eugenics, 1910–1935," *Long Island Historical Journal* 14, 1–2 (2001): 1–14.

5. See www.westland.net/coneyisland/articles/freaks.htm.

6. Such structural containment and separation within the setting of an optical regime was in line with contemporary trends in the building of prisons and animal zoos. Compare Michel Foucault, *Surveiller et punir: Naissance de la Prison* (Paris: Gallimard, 1975).

7. Mikhail Bakhtin. *Rabelais and His World* (Bloomington: Indiana University Press, 1993).

8. Roberto Bolaño, *The Third Reich* (New York: Farrar, Straus and Giroux, 2011), 20.

9. William Faulkner, *Light in August* (New York: Random House, 1959), 345–46.

10. Turning Victor Hugo's novel into a film brought a number of problems, one of which was to adapt for a visual medium like film a story whose focus was on the inner life of a character behind a mask, incapable of expressing inner emotions. On this problem, see Mireille Gamel, "L'homme qui rit à l'écran: Du bon usage de l'infidélité," http://groupugo.div.jussieu.fr /groupugo/03–04–26gamel.htm.

One enduring echo of Paul Leni's film adaptation in American mass culture is the face of the Joker in the *Batman* series of comic books, styled after Conrad Veidt's makeup.

11. James Baldwin, "The Last Interview," in Quincy Troupe, ed., *James Baldwin: The Legacy* (New York: Simon and Schuster, 1989), 193.

12. A. Trachtenberg, *Reading American Photographs: Images as History, Mathew Brady to Walker Evans* (New York: Hill and Wang, 1989), ch. I, 21–71.

13. Marianne Hirsch, *Family Frames: Photography, Narrative and Postmemory* (Cambridge: Harvard university Press, 1997), 103.

14. Doon Arbus and Marvin Israel, eds., *Diane Arbus: An Aperture Monograph* (New York: Aperture Foundation, 1972), 15. William Todd Schultz,

An Emergency in Slow Motion: The Inner Life of Diane Arbus (London: Bloomsbury, 2011).

15. Robert Bogdan, *Picturing Disability: Beggar, Freak, Citizen, and Other Photographic Rhetoric* (Syracuse, NY: Syracuse University Press, 2012).

16. See http://libcom.org/library/ending-war-inventing-movement-may day-1971.

17. If Browning's film can be seen as an invitation to conceive of freaks as fellow human beings, the last part of its narrative seems to undermine this message. In the terrible revenge meted out to Cleo, the freaks seem to confirm the classic view of them as threatening and scary creatures. For an enlightening reading of inner contradictions in the film's story, see Joan Hawkins, "'One of Us': Tod Browning's *Freaks*," in Rosemary Garland Thompson, ed., *Freakery: Spectacles of the Extraordinary Body* (New York: New York University Press, 1996), 265–76.

18. Amy Louise Wood, *Lynching and Spectacle: Witnessing Racial Violence in America, 1890–1940* (Chapel Hill: University of North Carolina Press, 2009).

19. For a grisly collection of such photographs, see James Allen et al., *Without Sanctuary: Lynching Photography in America* (Santa Fe, NM: Twin Palms Publishers, 2000).

20. The photograph is available on http://gutenberg.spiegel.de/gutenb /holitsch/amerikah/bilder/s367.jpg.

21. Martin Goldsmith, *The Inextinguishable Symphony: A True Story of Music and Love in Nazi Germany* (New York: John Wiley and Sons, 2000).

22. Kurt Baschwitz, *Du und die Masse: Studien zu einer exakten Massenpsychologie* (Amsterdam: Feikema, Carelsen en Co., 1938), ch. 18.

23. Wood, *Lynching and Spectacle*, 238.

24. Richard Raskin, *A Child at Gunpoint: A Case Study in the Life of a Photo* (Aarhus: Aarhus University Press, 2004). Chapter II reprints and discusses all fifty-three photographs in the two surviving copies of the document. The "Dregs of Humanity" photograph is #12 from the collection.

25. B. Zelizer, *About to Die: How News Images Move the Public* (Oxford: Oxford University Press, 2010), 138.

Chapter 7. American Responses to the Holocaust: Atrocity Photographs as Nomadic Objects

1. Never mind that upon closer scrutiny the boy most likely squinted his eyes against the sun, which, judging by the shadow his small body casts, the boy was facing. He must have been looking at the photographer.

2. Barbie Zelizer, *Remembering to Forget: Holocaust Memory through the Camera's Eye* (Chicago: University of Chicago Press, 1998), 104–5.

3. Werner Sollors, "Hard on the Eyes: A Photographer and His Subject," (unpublished lecture, Amsterdam, January 17, 2011).

4. Alex Ross, *The Rest Is Noise: Listening to the Twentieth Century* (New York: Farrar, Straus and Giroux, 2007), 497.

5. Aad Wagenaar, *Settela: Het meisje heeft haar naam terug* (The Girl Has Her Name Back) (Hilversum: Just Publishers, 1995), published with an accompanying DVD, containing both the original 1944 Westerbork film and the documentary by Cherry Duyns, *Settela: Gezicht van het verleden* (Face of the Past), broadcast initially by VPRO Television in 1996.

6. Richard Raskin, *A Child at Gunpoint: A Case Study in the Life of a Photo* (Aarhus: Aarhus University Press, 2004); Frédéric Rousseau, *L'enfant juif de Varsovie: Histoire d'une photographie* (Paris: Editions de Seuil, 2009).

7. Jean Back and Viktoria Schmidt-Linsenhoff, eds., *The Family of Man 1955–2001, Humanism and Postmodernism: A Reappraisal of the Photo Exhibition by Edward Steichen* (Marburg: Jonas Verlag, 2004).

8. A key role here was played by American historian Eric J. Sandeen. See his *Exhibition: The Family of Man and 1950s America* (Albuquerque: University of New Mexico Press, 1995).

See also Eric J. Sandeen, *Picturing an Exhibition: The Family of Man and 1950s America* (Albuquerque: University of New Mexico Press, 1995).

9. See Back and Linsenhoff, *The Family of Man 1955–2001*.

10. Viktoria Schmidt-Linsenhoff, "Denied Images," in Back and Schmidt-Linsenhoff, *The Family of Man 1955–2001*, 80–100. The quotation is from the introduction, p. 11.

11. Frédéric Rousseau discusses this initial Israeli reluctance in his *L'enfant juif de Varsovie*, 124ff.

12. Viktoria Schmidt-Linsenhoff, "Denied Images," 95.

13. Even a historian like Hasia Diner, while assembling an impressive array of evidence against the myth of silence on the subject of the Holocaust, overlooks Steichen's public stance. Compare Hasia Diner, *We Remember with Reverence and Love: American Jews and the Myth of Silence after the Holocaust, 1945–1962* (New York: New York University Press, 2009).

14. Anne Swartz tells the story of the response, angered or supportive, to Schechner's work in New York. Anne Swartz, "There Are Many Sides to Every Story: Alan Schechner Looks at the Holocaust," *Fine Art Forum* (April 2002).

15. The work is presented on the following website: www.dottycommies
.com/holocaust10.html The artist, Alan Schechner, served in the Israeli army
from 1981 to 1983 with active duty both in the Occupied Territories and
Lebanon. The work described here is both a "stand alone" project in itself,
and also used in "Dialog," a collaboration between Schechner and Palestinian artist Rana Bishara.

Chapter 8. Barack Hussein Obama: Two Portrait Sketches

1. In an interview with Gary Younge, *Guardian Weekly* (August 20,
2007). Patterson's reflections on the lukewarm initial support for Obama's
presidential candidacy among America's black population led him to speak
of "black nativism." See Orlando Patterson, "The New Black Nativism,"
Time Magazine, February 8, 2007.

2. J. W. Schulte Nordholt, *Het volk dat in duisternis wandelt: De ge-
schiedenis van de negers in Amerika* (Deventer: Van Loghum Slaterus, 1968).

3. Obama speech, "A More Perfect Union," Constitution Center, Philadelphia, March 18, 2008, www.huffingtonpost.com/2008/03/18/obama-race
-speech-read-th_n_92077.html.

4. Letter to Horace Greeley, August 22, 1862.

5. Sacvan Bercovitch, *The American Jeremiad* (Madison: University of
Wisconsin Press, 1978).

6. Obama Cairo speech, video and full text, www.huffingtonpost.com
/2009/06/04/obama-speech-in-cairo-vid_n_211215.html.

7. September 19, 2010, www.reuters.com/article/idUSTRE68I03S20100919.

8. James T. Kloppenberg, in his *Reading Obama,* looks at Obama's writing
and record of public speech to do for Obama what Obama does for himself:
demonstrating the extent to which he as a politician and a statesman is rooted
in an American political and intellectual tradition. See Kloppenberg, *Reading Obama: Dreams, Hope, and the American Political Tradition* (Princeton: Princeton University Press, 2010). See also Susan Schulten, "Barack
Obama, Abraham Lincoln, and John Dewey," *Denver University Law Review* 86 (2009), http://law.du.edu/documents/denver-university-law-review
/schulten.pdf.

9. See www.huffingtonpost.com/2008/07/24/obama-in-berlin-video-of_n
_114771.html.

10. See www.scribd.com/doc/4107132/Barack-Obama-on-Homeland
-Security. This is an electoral campaign document, summarizing Obama's
views of the Homeland Security counterterrorism apparatus and strategy.
It contains telling policy projects that today, in the eyes of critics, seem to

be honored in the breach. Among the promises made we find the following: "Obama also would restore habeas corpus so that those who pose a danger are swiftly tried and brought to justice and those who do not have sufficient due process to ensure that we are not wrongfully denying them their liberty."

11. Lawrence Goodwyn, *The Populist Moment: A Short History of the Agrarian Revolt in America* (Oxford: Oxford University Press, 1978), xiii.

12. Garry Wills, *Lincoln at Gettysburg: The Words That Remade America* (New York: Touchstone, 1992).

13. The CNN/Opinion Research Corporation poll was conducted July 16–21, 2011, with 1,018 adult Americans questioned by telephone. The survey's overall sampling error is plus or minus three percentage points.

14. "We believe that the best of America is in these small towns that we get to visit, and in these wonderful little pockets of what I call the real America." Greensboro, NC, October 16, 2008, http://voices.washington post.com/44/2008/10/to-avoid-being-depressed-palin.html?hpid=topnews.

15. Orlando Patterson, "Race and Diversity in the Age of Obama," *New York Times Sunday Book Review* (August 14, 2009), www.nytimes.com /2009/08/16/books/review/Patterson-t.html. See also Patterson, "The New Black Nativism," *Time Magazine* (February 8, 2007).

16. Barack Obama, *Dreams from My Father: A Story of Race and Inheritance* (New York: Times Books, 1995); Barack Obama, *The Audacity of Hope: Thoughts on Reclaiming the American Dream* (New York: Crown Publishers, 2006); "2004 Democratic National Convention Keynote Address," delivered July 27, 2004, Fleet Center, Boston, www.youtube.com /watch?v=eWynt87PaJo.

17. See Kloppenberg, *Reading Obama*. For a similar, article-length argument, see Schulten, "Barack Obama, Abraham Lincoln, and John Dewey."

18. Kloppenberg, *Reading Obama*, http://harvardmagazine.com/2010 /11/a-nation-arguing-with-its-conscience?page=all#, p. 2.

19. On consensus history, see M. J. Morton, *The Terrors of Ideological Politics: Liberal Historians in a Conservative Mood* (Cleveland, OH: Case Western Reserve University Press, 1972). See also Richard H. Pells, *The Liberal Mind in a Conservative Age: American Intellectuals in the 1940s & 1950s* (New York: Harper and Row, 1985).

Chapter 9. Obama and the Paradox of American Global Power: Dreams of Democracy and the Imperial Imperative

1. Arthur M. Schlesinger, *The Imperial Presidency* (New York: Houghton Mifflin, 1973).

2. Jennifer van Bergen, "The Unitary Executive: Is the Doctrine behind the Bush Presidency Consistent with a Democratic State? http://writ.news .findlaw.com/commentary/20060109_bergen.html;

Jennifer van Bergen, *The Twilight of Democracy: The Bush Plan for America* (Monroe, ME: Common Courage Press, 2004).

3. Glenn Greenwald, "Obama Wins the Right to Detain People with No Habeas Review," May 23, 2010, www.informationclearinghouse.info/article 25517.htm.

4. This is a point raised by Robert Naiman ("An Open Letter to Liberal Supporters of the Libya War," www.huffingtonpost.com/robert-naiman /an-open-letter-to-liberal_b_841505.html), in his response to Juan Cole's "An Open Letter to the Left on Libya," which is generally supportive of the war (www.juancole.com/2011/03/an-open-letter-to-the-left-on-libya.html). Naiman uses strong language and speaks of a power grab by the executive.

5. To get to this linguistic stretch President Obama had had to overrule the lawyers in the Justice and Defense departments and turn to more pliant ones in the White House and State Department. Bruce Ackerman, a professor of law and political science at Yale, said in the *New York Times* that this could open the way for "even more blatant acts of presidential war-making in the decades ahead"; see "Legal Acrobatics, Illegal War," www.nytimes .com/2011/06/21/opinion/21Ackerman.html.

6. Following a sustained public outcry, culminating in a public letter over the signature of more than 250 top legal scholars, including Laurence Tribe, a Harvard professor who had taught Obama constitutional law, and published in the *New York Review of Books,* Manning was transferred to a more normal detention regime; see *New York Review of Books* 58, 5 (May 12–25, 2011): 62.

7. *New York Review of Books* (May 27, 2010): 17.

8. Maeva Marcus, *Truman and the Steel Seizure Case: The Limits of Presidential Power* (New York: Columbia University Press, 1977).

9. Gabriel Schoenfeld, "Barack Obama: Defender of State Secrets," *Wall Street Journal,* Thursday, September 30, 2010, 17.

10. Colin Powell's words of praise and endorsement can still be heard on the Internet: www.youtube.com/watch?v=T_NMZv6Vfh8. It is an excerpt from NBC's *Meet the Press*, October 19, 2008.

11. For a critical review of alternative policies, see Juan Cole, *Engaging the Muslim World* (New York: Palgrave MacMillan, 2009).

12. "But I'm the decider, and I decide what is best." Words spoken on the White House Lawn, April 18, 2006.

13. For the text of Reagan's "Evil Empire Speech," see www.national center.org/ReaganEvilEmpire1983.html.

14. President Jimmy Carter, Commencement Speech given at Notre Dame University, June 1977, http://teachingamericanhistory.org/library/index.asp?document=727.

15. See http://my.barackobama.com/page/content/fpccga.

16. For an enlightening revisit of Eisenhower's farewell speech, see Andrew J. Bacevich, "The Tyranny of Defense Inc.," *Atlantic* (January/February 2011), www.theatlantic.com/magazine/archive/2011/01/the-tyranny-of-defense-inc/8342/.

17. See www.justice.gov/iso/opa/ag/speeches/2012/ag-speech-1203051.html.

18. In an interview on CNN, Wednesday, September 5, 2012, Obama himself briefly went into the criteria used in drone warfare. Obama told CNN that a terror suspect had to pass five tests before the administration would allow him to be taken out by a drone. "Drones are one tool that we use, and our criteria for using them is very tight and very strict," the president said.

1. "It has to be a target that is authorized by our laws."
2. "It has to be a threat that is serious and not speculative."
3. "It has to be a situation in which we can't capture the individual before they move forward on some sort of operational plot against the United States."
4. "We've got to make sure that in whatever operations we conduct, we are very careful about avoiding civilian casualties."
5. "That while there is a legal justification for us to try and stop [American citizens] from carrying out plots . . . they are subject to the protections of the Constitution and due process."

For a brief discussion of these points see www.wired.com/dangerroom/2012/09/obama-drone/

19. Aaron B. O'Connell, "The Permanent Militarization of America," *New York Times*, Opinion pages, November 4, 2012, www.nytimes.com/2012/11/05/opinion/the-permanent-militarization-of-america.html?pagewanted=all&_r=0.

Tom Engelhardt, *The United States of Fear* (Chicago: Haymarket Books, 2011)

20. David Wise and Thomas B. Ross, *The Invisible Government* (New York: Random House, 1964), 3.

21. Ibid., 219.

22. Tom Junod, "The Lethal Presidency of Barack Obama," *Esquire* (August 2012), www.esquire.com/features/obama-lethal-presidency-0812.

23. Chalmers H. Johnson, "America's Empire of Bases," January 15, 2004, www.commondreams.org/views04/0115–08.htm.

Ch. H. Johnson, *The Sorrows of Empire: Militarism, Secrecy, and the End of the Republic* (New York: Henry Holt, 2004).

Chapter 10. Taking Exception

1. Sacvan Bercovitch, *The American Jeremiad* (Madison: University of Wisconsin Press, 1978).

2. "The Big Lie," The Daily Dish, *Atlantic* (November 9, 2010).

3. C. Vann Woodward, *The Burden of Southern History* (Baton Rouge: Louisiana State University Press, 1993); C. Vann Woodward, *American Counterpoint: Slavery and Racism in the North-South Dialogue* (Boston: Little, Brown and Company, 1964).

4. S. M. Lipset, *American Exceptionalism: A Double-Edged Sword* (New York: W. W. Norton and Company, 1997).

5. Daniel T. Rodgers, "Exceptionalism," in Anthony Molho and Gordon S. Wood, eds., *Imagined Histories: American Historians Interpret the Past* (Princeton: Princeton University Press, 1998), 22–23.

6. Daniel T. Rodgers, *Atlantic Crossings: Social Politics in a Progressive Age* (Cambridge: Harvard University Press, 1998).

7. Thomas Bender, ed., *Rethinking American History in a Global Age* (Berkeley: University of California Press, 2002); David Thelen, *The Nation and Beyond*, a special issue of *The Journal of American History* 86, 3 (December 1999). I had the good fortune to be involved in both projects.

8. Bender, *Rethinking American History in a Global Age,* vii.

9. Alan Wolfe, "Anti-American Studies," *New Republic* (February 10, 2003). In his piece, Wolfe reviewed Pease and Wiegman, eds., *The Futures of American Studies;* John Carlos Rowe, *The New American Studies;* and David Noble, *Death of a Nation: American Culture and the End of Exceptionalism.*

10. Donald Pease, "Rethinking 'American Studies after US Exceptionalism,'" 22, http://alh.oxfordjournals.org/content/21/1/19.full.

INDEX